TERRIBLE *BUT* TRUE

Awful Events in American History

by **Dinah Williams**

Scholastic Inc.

To my wonderful and weird family, who make me feel normal. —D.W.

Text copyright © 2016 by Dinah Dunn

All rights reserved. Published by Scholastic Inc.,
Publishers since 1920. SCHOLASTIC and associated logos
are trademarks and/or registered trademarks of Scholastic Inc.

ISBN 978-0-545-90972-3

10 9 8 7 6 5 4 3 2   16 17 18 19 20

Printed in the U.S.A. 23

First edition, September 2016

Book design by Nancy Sabato
Photo research by Emily Teresa

CONTENTS

KEY:

 Adventurer ⬤ Leader ⬤ Progress

⬤ Battle ⬤ Medical ⬤ Riot

⬤ Disaster

INTRODUCTION

When I was in school, history bored me. I'd zone out on what seemed like a never-ending list of dates until the bell finally rang to change classes.

I could never get enough of books, though, because they contained stories about people—how they felt, what they did, how they lived. I didn't realize that history could be equally interesting until I first learned about the *General Slocum* disaster. Never heard of it? Neither had I.

In June 1904, a steamboat full of people was heading up the East River in New York City to a picnic. Suddenly a fire broke out. The desperate captain tried to make it to North Brother Island a mile away, but the speed just fanned the fire. One newspaper at the time described it as "a spectacle of horror beyond words to express—a great vessel all in flames, sweeping forward in the sunlight, within sight of the crowded city, while her helpless, screaming hundreds were roasted alive or swallowed up in waves."

With more than one thousand dead, the *General Slocum* was New York's worst disaster until 9/11. I couldn't believe I knew nothing about a tragedy that

The horrific fire aboard the General Slocum.

happened only twenty miles from my house, on a river I crossed every day on my way to work. I spent hours reading accounts from rescuers and reporters and survivors—all of the people who lived through that awful day. And that's when history became real to me.

With *Terrible but True*, I want to introduce you to some of the weird, tragic, and altogether awful stories hiding in plain sight in America's past. From tornadoes to fires to a swarm of a billion locusts, you'll find plenty of disasters in this book, along with mesmerizing stories of gruesome deaths by disease. Any battle or war is filled with slaughter and despair, but in *Terrible but True* you'll read about the ones that were most shocking or unusual. There are also dreadful tales

Hundreds of dead from the General Slocum *in the temporary morgue.*

of bloody riots, assassinations, and massacres. Anything that left me stunned—that caused me to grab someone and say, "Can you believe this actually happened?"—made the cut.

My hope is that by the time you finish this book, you won't be bored by history. And maybe you'll want to learn just a little bit more.

PART I: REVOLUTIONARY WAR
AND THE NEW NATION (1764–1828)

1770 Boston Massacre

Boston Tea Party **1773**

1775 First shots fired at Lexington and Concord; George Washington takes command of new Continental army

Declaration of Independence signed **1776**

1777 British defeated at Saratoga

Benedict Arnold treason uncovered **1780**

1781 American victory at Yorktown, leading to British surrender

Peace treaty signed in Paris **1783**

1789 George Washington inaugurated as president of the United States

John Adams begins term as president **1797**

Thomas Jefferson begins term as president **1801**

1803 Louisiana Purchase

Lewis and Clark explore the Louisiana Territory **1804**

1808 Slave trade with Africa ended

James Madison begins term as president **1809**

1812 War with England begins

Treaty of Ghent ends war with England **1814**

1817 James Monroe begins term as president

John Quincy Adams begins term as president **1825**

The Disease-Ridden Prison Ships
OF REVOLUTIONARY
THE WAR

Ebenezer Fox, who survived being imprisoned on the Jersey, *wrote of being "exposed to contagion; in contact with disease, and surrounded with the horrors of sickness and death."*

During the Revolutionary War, three times as many Americans died in British jails and on prison ships than those who died in battle. As many as 11,500 died due to terrible and filthy conditions on sixteen ships in New York Harbor, which was close to the British headquarters during the war. The vessels, known as hulks, were anchored in the Hudson and East Rivers. They housed prisoners from all thirteen colonies, as well as other countries.

General Jeremiah Johnson, who was a young boy living in Brooklyn during the war, described the conditions: **"Bad provisions, bad water, and scanted rations were dealt to the prisoners. No medical men attended the sick, disease reigned unrelieved, and hundreds died from pestilence, or were starved, on board this floating prison."** Smallpox and other diseases were widespread. Many of the dead were dumped in mass graves on the northwest shore of Brooklyn, while others were thrown overboard.

Captain Thomas Dring, a prisoner aboard the hulk *Jersey*, described being locked in the hold at night: "Silence was a stranger to our dark abode. There were continual noises during the night. The groans of the sick and the dying; the curses poured out by the weary and exhausted upon our inhuman keepers; the restlessness caused by the suffocating heat and the confined and poisonous air, mingled with the wild and incoherent ravings of delirium, were the sounds which, every night, were raised around us in all directions."

The ships were so disgusting that, after the war was over, many were just abandoned to rot.

Starvation and food poisoning killed many prisoners. The rations they did receive were barely fit to eat, with moldy worm-filled biscuits and rancid beef and butter.

In a winter that George Washington described as "intensely cold and freezing," the soldiers not only had to battle the elements but starvation as well.

THE WORST WINTER EVER

While history books detail the winter horrors suffered by the American Continental army in its camp at Valley Forge, Pennsylvania, a more terrible winter happened two years later in 1779–1780. Record-setting snowfalls and freezing temperatures were thought to be the worst in four hundred years. More than seven thousand soldiers wintered with George Washington in log cabins in Morristown, New Jersey.

Army surgeon James Thacher wrote in his journal, "No man could endure its violence many minutes without danger of his life . . . When the storm subsided, the snow was from four to six feet deep . . . [Soldiers were] buried like sheep under the snow." They had few clothes and even less food. Private Joseph Plumb Martin later wrote of his time in Morristown that "we were absolutely, literally starved . . . I did not put a single morsel . . . into my mouth for four days and as many nights, except a little black birch bark, which I gnawed off a stick of wood . . . I saw several of the men roast their old shoes and eat them."

BENEDICT ARNOLD'S Long, Deadly March

Benedict Arnold was at first considered a hero and a "fighting general" by George Washington.

In the early years of the Revolutionary War between the thirteen American colonies and Great Britain, Congress voted to send an army into the British colony of Canada to make it a "fourteenth colony." Benedict Arnold's mission was to invade the Canadian province of Quebec and capture its capital, Quebec City. In mid-September 1775, together with 1,100 men, Colonel Arnold left Cambridge, Massachusetts, and began an insanely long march north through the uncharted wilderness of Maine, facing freezing rain, snow, starvation, and really leaky boats.

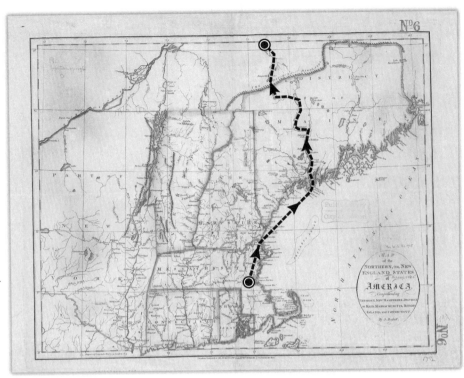

A 1795 map of New England showing Arnold's treacherous journey.

In a letter from November 27, 1775, Arnold later described his horrible journey: "In about eight weeks we completed a march of near six hundred miles, not to be paralleled in history, the men having, with the greatest fortitude and perseverance hauled their bateaux [boats] up rapid streams, being obliged [forced] to wade almost the whole way near one hundred eighty miles, carried them on their shoulders near forty miles, over hills, swamps, and bogs almost impenetrable." On top of heavy loads and dense wilderness, the troops were also near starving.

Soldier Simon Forbes later wrote, "I was told that some of the soldiers, who ate their whole allowance the morning after our provisions were divided, were obliged, in order to sustain life, to eat their dogs, cartridge-boxes, old shoes, and clothes. A number

perished [died] **by reason of hunger, fatigue, and cold. The next season, when returning home, I saw their bleaching bones."** Arnold himself wrote that his men "were almost naked, barefooted, and much fatigued." Nearly two hundred men died on the way to Canada and roughly one-third of the original group turned back before getting there.

Unfortunately, the deadly trip was not successful. Together with American troops who had traveled north from Lake Champlain to help, Arnold's troops attacked Quebec City, but failed to conquer it. The defeated Americans retreated south to Fort Ticonderoga in New York.

BITTER BENEDICT

Though a failure, Arnold's invasion of Quebec made him an American hero and he was eventually promoted to the rank of brigadier general. However, he was seriously wounded twice and publicly taken to court over some small issues. Arnold grew angry. He felt he deserved more promotions, more fame, more respect, and more money. In 1780 he asked for the position of commander of West Point, an important fort on the Hudson River in New York. In a secret plot with the British, once he was the commander, Arnold planned to surrender the fort to them. In return he would receive a large amount of money. The plot was discovered before he could carry it out and Arnold escaped to Britain. George Washington called his actions "treason of the blackest dye" and had every mention of Arnold's heroics erased from the public record. Today, Arnold's name is still a synonym for "traitor."

John André of the British Army was captured carrying Benedict Arnold's map of West Point and was executed by hanging for being a spy.

DANIEL BOONE'S Rotten Luck

Daniel Boone: fearless or foolish?

Civilization in colonial America was mostly located in cities along the Atlantic coast. There were very few settlements inland, and the only non-native peoples living and traveling west of the Appalachian Mountains were fur traders and hunters, and explorers known as frontiersmen. As they were traveling through Indian territory, confrontations were inevitable.

In May 1769, frontiersman Daniel Boone, accompanied by five other men, blazed a trail from their homes in western North Carolina into territory that later would become Tennessee and Kentucky. **Boone was captured twice by Indians who told him that he had no right traveling in land that belonged to them. The first time he was set free after receiving a warning, and the second time he escaped.** Boone continued his exploration, returning home in 1771.

Two years later Boone and about fifty other men attempted to build a settlement in Kentucky. However, they were attacked by Indians and six were killed, including Boone's son James. Then in 1775 he was hired to blaze a path through the Cumberland Gap in the Appalachian Mountains, a path from Virginia to central Kentucky that came to be called the Wilderness Trail. There, at the Kentucky River, he founded Boone's Station (later Boonesborough). Trouble soon followed.

Fort Boonesborough, Kentucky, in April 1775.

In 1776, Boone's daughter Jemima was out with two girls floating in a canoe when they were kidnapped by Shawnee and Cherokee Indians. Boone quickly gathered a rescue party and followed them. After killing a few of the kidnappers, they were able to rescue the girls.

The next year Boone's Station was attacked by the Shawnee. Boone was shot in the ankle but was pulled to safety before he could be killed. Then in February 1778 he was captured by the Shawnee while hunting. Outnumbered and too old to run, he surrendered and was brought to their main village, Old Chillicothe. **Boone was given the Shawnee name "Sheltowee," or "Big Turtle," because he walked slowly and carried a big pack.** While he lived in relative comfort, he was always looking for ways to escape from his captors. When he saw the Indian men gathering in June to march against Boone's Station, he recalled, "I determined to escape the first opportunity. On the sixteenth, before sunrise, I departed in the most secret manner, and arrived at Boone's Station on the twentieth, after a journey of one hundred and sixty miles, during which I had but one meal." He arrived before the Shawnee and quickly helped build up the fort's defenses.

The Indians arrived and surrounded the fort where the settlers were sheltered, cutting them off from supplies. During the battle, thirty-seven Indians were killed along with two settlers. The fighting was fierce, and in the end, the Shawnee retreated.

Despite the threat of further attacks, Boone continued to live

in the area with friends and family, including his brother Ned. One day in 1780, while they were out collecting salt, Ned was shot and killed by Indians. Two years later Boone fought against the Indians again at the Battle of Blue Licks. There his son Israel was killed.

Even though Boone was constantly getting into scrapes, he miraculously managed to survive multiple attacks. He was finally killed by old age in 1820 at eighty-five. His final words were believed to be,

"I'm going now. My time has come."

Davy Crockett

THE LIFE AND DEATH OF DAVY CROCKETT

David Crockett, like Daniel Boone, was a frontiersman known for his hunting ability. He once shot more than one hundred bears in a single year! A veteran of the War of 1812 and a three-time Congressman from Tennessee, Crockett was beloved for his ability to tell a good tale, such as the time he lost his pants on the Mississippi River! When he failed to win the congressional election of 1835, he decided to go fight for Texas independence.

Crockett is probably best known for his heroic death at the Alamo in Texas in 1836. He is quoted in 1875's *David Crockett: His Life and Adventures* as saying, "I know not whether, in the eyes of the world, a brilliant death is not preferred to an obscure life of rectitude. Most men are remembered as they died, and not as they lived." This may be why he is still so well known today!

Daniel Boone's log cabin in High Bridge, Kentucky.

The Butcher of
BUFORD'S
MASSACRE

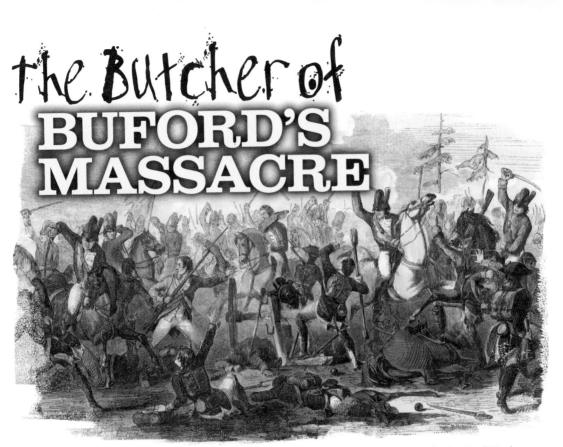

Buford's Massacre was also known as the Battle of Waxhaws.

May 29, 1780, Lancaster County, South Carolina. In the middle of the Revolutionary War, Banastre Tarleton's British cavalry caught up with Abraham Buford's American troops. Tarleton wrote Buford a message, demanding his surrender or "the blood be upon your head." Buford refused, writing back, "I reject your proposals and shall defend myself to the last extremity." Tarleton took him at his word. His troops killed 113 men, severely wounded 147 others, and took the remaining 53 men prisoner. Tarleton lost only five men. But was this a massacre or a battle? Depends who you ask.

One version of the events told at the time had Buford surrendering after the battle began and Tarleton's men viciously slaughtering the helpless troops. Buford rode to safety while he said many of his men

"were killed after they had lain down their arms."

Tarleton described his version in a letter to General Cornwallis: As the Americans were attempting to surrender, his horse was shot out from under him. His troops thought Tarleton was dead, so they attacked the Americans in revenge. Either way, it was a bloodbath.

American captain John Stokes was one of the soldiers who was attacked while he was already down. Badly wounded, Stokes had a gash on his forehead, stabbings across his arms, and one of his fingers cut off. When asked by the British if he wanted to surrender, he said, **"I have not, nor do I mean to ask it; finish me as soon as possible,"** and then was stabbed twice with a bayonet. But Stokes survived and was kept as a prisoner of the British until the end of the war in 1783.

BLOODY BAN, THE MOST HATED BRITISH OFFICER IN AMERICA

When Commander Banastre Tarleton's men slaughtered American troops at Waxhaws, he became known as "Bloody Ban" or simply "The Butcher." "Tarleton's quarter" became synonymous with "no surrender," meaning no prisoners taken—all soldiers would just be killed. Americans hated him, and with good reason. When American general Richard Richardson's widow warned American officer Francis Marlon that Tarleton was on his way so Marlon could escape, in 1780, Tarleton was furious. He was said to have ordered the dead body of Richardson dug up, then he burned down Richardson's house and beat his widow when she couldn't tell him where Marlon was headed. Tarleton's major defeat at the Battle of Cowpens, with approximately 100 killed and 229 wounded, thrilled American troops.

Corpse-Stealing Doctors
CAUSE A RIOT

Medical students in New York dug up bodies at night using wooden shovels, which were quieter than metal ones.

RIOT

How can you practice surgery if you don't have any bodies? This was a problem for early medical students, who were known to steal corpses, especially in the winter when the bodies would be preserved by the cold. The students often chose to steal from the graves of citizens who were poor, as there was a lower chance their family members would go to the police. The medical school at Columbia College in New York City was located near two cemeteries. Locals complained to authorities about the thefts but nothing had been done. Newspaper stories about the grave robbings fanned people's fury.

On April 16, 1788, a student at Columbia was dissecting an arm. He waved it out the window to a group of kids, saying jokingly that it was one of their mom's arms. A boy whose mother had recently died told his father, who checked her grave to find it coincidentally empty. Furious, he gathered a mob and they marched to the hospital. Colonel William Heth, in a letter to Virginia governor Edmund Randolph, wrote about what they found:

Grave robbers, also called resurrectionists, sometimes held bodies for ransom, insisting on payment from relatives before returning them.

"three fresh bodies—one, boiling in a kettle, and two others cut up."

News quickly spread and soon thousands of people surrounded the hospital. Physician James Thacher, who witnessed the riot, later wrote, "Some of the mob having forced their way into the dissecting room, **several human bodies were found in various states of mutilation [being cut up].**

Enraged at this discovery, they seized upon the fragments, as heads, legs, and arms, and exposed them from the windows and doors to public view." Authorities took the med students into custody to keep them safe. The militia, or state's army, was also called in to protect them when protesters began throwing bricks and rocks. Between five and twenty people were killed in the riot.

The New York Doctor's Riot is one of many "anatomy riots" that occurred between the 1760s and the 1850s throughout the United States.

In January 1789, the New York State Legislature put forward a law to prevent the disgusting practice of "digging up and removing for the purpose of dissection, dead bodies interred in cemeteries or burial places," with the punishment of being forced to stand in wooden shackles in the public square or being publicly whipped, fined, or imprisoned.

MAGGOT AND LEECH THERAPY

Before doctors discovered the drugs that help treat and cure certain diseases, they tried anything they thought might help. For thousands of years, both maggots and leeches were a common medical tool. Maggots eat dead skin and tissue, which enables doctors to get closer to healthy cells. They were used for burns, gangrene, and skin cancer. During the Civil War, Dr. J. F. Zacharias reported that, "Maggots . . . in a single day would clean a wound much better than any agents we had at our command."

A woman using leeches for bloodletting in 1638.

Leech saliva contains a blood thinner to prevent clots, and substances that reduce pain and swelling. They were attached to swollen areas of a patient's skin. Unfortunately, leeches got a bad reputation because for centuries doctors mistakenly believed that diseases were caused by "bad blood," which leeches were supposed to remove. Patients became weaker as the leeches continued to drain away blood. In extreme cases, patients would bleed to death.

Today, new science has recognized that both maggots and leeches can be effective treatments in some cases, and they may be making a medical comeback!

PHILADELPHIA'S
Yellow fever Plague

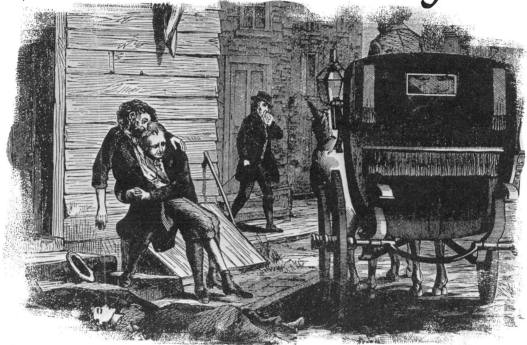

Carriages traveled through the streets of Philadelphia, picking up the dying and dead bodies.

Until the 1860s, when French chemist and biologist Louis Pasteur proved that germs and other microorganisms were the sources of disease, doctors did not know what caused illnesses such as yellow fever and cholera.

Yellow fever is a viral infection spread by mosquitoes.

Victims suffer aches and pains, a high fever, yellowing of the eyes and skin, and vomit black clots of blood.

The disease is believed to have originated in Africa, brought to North America as a result of the slave trade.

When yellow fever hit the nation's first capital, Philadelphia, in 1793, government leaders and many residents fled the city. George Washington wrote a friend that **"as Mrs. Washington was unwilling to leave me surrounded by the malignant fever which prevailed, I could not think of hazarding her and the children any longer by my continuance in the city, the house in which we lived being, in a manner, blockaded, by the disorder."**

Physician Benjamin Rush couldn't get enough help in caring for the sick and burying the dead. Mistakenly believing that all black people were immune to the disease, he asked members of the Free African Society for help. Absalom Jones, who later founded the first African Methodist Episcopal Church, volunteered. He teamed up with friend Richard Allen and began gathering the dead. They wrote: "A woman died, we were sent for to bury her, on our going into the house and taking the coffin in, a dear little innocent accosted us with, **'mamma is asleep, don't wake her'**; but when she saw us put her in the coffin, the distress of the child was so great that it almost overcame us."

The dead house on the Schuylkill River and 22nd Street in Philadelphia was used to store bodies during the yellow fever epidemic.

Nearly nine percent of the city's fifty-five thousand residents died from yellow fever. When the weather cooled, the mosquitoes died, slowing the spread of the disease. But it would come back again just as strong in the 1800s.

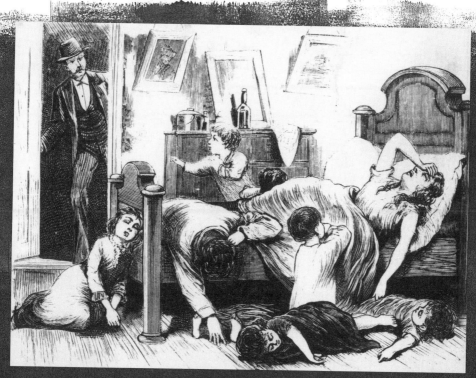

Entire families could be overcome by deadly diseases.

THE DEADLIEST NINETEENTH-CENTURY YELLOW FEVER AND CHOLERA EPIDEMICS IN THE UNITED STATES

Outside of yellow fever, the other big killer of the nineteenth century was cholera, a bacterial infection that causes such terrible diarrhea that it kills you. These were the five biggest epidemics of the nineteenth century:

1878 - Lower Mississippi Valley yellow fever death toll: 13,000+

1853 - New Orleans yellow fever death toll: 7,790+

1848 - New York City cholera death toll: 5,000

1832 - New Orleans cholera death toll: 4,340

1867 - New Orleans yellow fever death toll: 3,093

THE OHIO RIVER'S Most Vicious Pirate

Samuel Mason

How did a Revolutionary War hero and respected justice of the peace become a vicious pirate and wanted desperado? It's hard to say what drove Samuel Mason to a life of crime. During the Revolutionary War, he was a captain in the Virginia militia. After the war he moved to Pennsylvania, where he was both a peacekeeper and a judge. Mason was married and thought to have had six sons and four daughters. But he had some money problems, and in 1785 his farm was sold to pay off debts.

Mason moved his family to Kentucky and by the 1790s he was living the life of a pirate. He recruited fellow criminals and based his operation out of Cave-in-Rock on the Illinois shore of the Ohio River. There he'd invite river travelers to stop.

While they had refreshments, his men would secretly search their boat's cargo. If there were valuables, he and his men would rob the boat after the travelers had journeyed farther down the river. In 1799 his gang moved downriver to Mississippi, where the governor soon tired of Mason's thieving ways and offered a reward for his capture.

In January 1803 Mason was arrested in Missouri. **Although he claimed to be a farmer, authorities were unconvinced when they found seven thousand dollars and twenty human scalps in his baggage.**

In March, as he was being transported back to Mississippi by boat, Mason escaped. A letter written at the time stated that he threw off his irons, "seized the guns belonging to the boat, and fired upon the guard. Captain McCoy, hearing the alarm, ran out of the cabin, [and] old Mason instantly shot him through the breast and shoulder; [McCoy] with determined bravery of a soldier, though scarcely able to stand, shot him in the head. **Mason fell and rose, fell and rose again, and although in a gore of blood . . . drove off McCoy's party and kept possession of the boat till evening.**"

Boats on the Ohio River passing Cave-in-Rock, which is now thought to be haunted by ghosts of the pirates' victims.

The governor offered more money for his recapture, which proved too much temptation for Mason's own gang. Two bandits brought in Mason's head with hopes of collecting the reward, but were recognized as criminals themselves, and were arrested and hanged.

No image of the Harpe brothers exists but Micajah was said to be hulking and tall, and carried a large, head-splitting tomahawk. Wiley was smaller with red hair, but was said to be just as vicious.

AMERICA'S FIRST SERIAL KILLERS

Cave-in-Rock hosted a number of outlaws, none more vicious than cousins Micajah and Wiley Harpe. They fought with the British during the American Revolution and with the Indians during the frontier wars. They kidnapped women to be their wives. But it was murder that made them notorious. In the late 1790s they were thought to have killed more than twenty people in Kentucky and Tennessee, beginning with a murder at Hughes Tavern, near Knoxville. While the motive initially appeared to be robbery, the state of the dead bodies told a different story. The Harpes killed babies for crying and mothers for screaming. They proved too awful even for the Mason gang, whose members asked them to leave Cave-in-Rock after they stripped and blindfolded a man they robbed, tied him to a horse, and chased the horse off a cliff. In 1799 the law finally caught up with Micajah, who was shot while trying to escape. Wiley was caught in 1804, when he was one of the criminals recognized for bringing in the head of Samuel Mason! Both of their heads were cut off and displayed on posts as a warning to future outlaws.

GEORGE WASHINGTON, Nearly Superhuman, Killed by a Sore throat

A friend of Washington once described him: "His movements and gestures are graceful, his walk majestic, and he is a splendid horseman."

The fact that George Washington lived to the age of sixty-seven is something of a miracle. While that wasn't a particularly old age at the time, Washington survived dozens of things that had easily felled other men.

Though he was more than six feet tall and physically strong, Washington suffered a long string of illnesses. **Before reaching age twenty-one, he had diphtheria, tuberculosis, smallpox, malaria, and dysentery, all of which could have killed him.**

His brush with smallpox left him immune to the disease and was the reason he pushed to have American troops vaccinated during the Revolutionary War.

Before the Constitutional Convention, in 1787, he wrote in a letter, "I have of late been so much afflicted with a rheumatic complaint in my shoulder that at times I am hardly able to raise my hand to my head, or turn myself in bed." As president, he was bedridden for more than a month in 1789 with a tumor on his thigh that was so painful he told his aide, "I know it is very doubtful whether ever I shall arise from this bed and God knows it is perfectly indifferent to me whether I do or not." He eventually regained his strength, only to suffer from pneumonia in 1790.

On the battlefield Washington was just as lucky to survive. In 1755 he was an aide to British General Edmond Braddock. During the Battle of Monongahela, he had

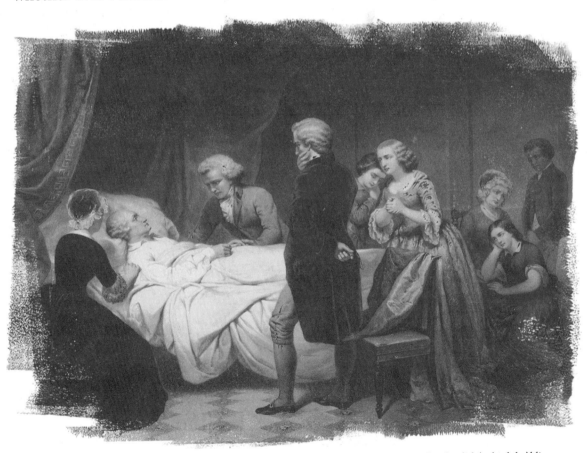

Doctors tried to save Washington with bloodletting, a common cure at the time, but he didn't think he'd live. Washington said, "Doctor, I die hard; but I am not afraid to go . . . my breath can not last long."

two horses shot out from under him and had four musket balls tear through his coat. To rally troops against the British during the Battle of Princeton, in 1777, he personally led the counterattack, shouting, "Parade with us my brave fellows! There is but a handful of the enemy and we shall have them directly!" A young officer at the Battle of Princeton wrote,

"I saw him brave all the dangers of the field . . . with a thousand deaths flying around him."

Having dodged bullets both literally and figuratively throughout his life, it is shocking that a man so lucky was killed by a sore throat. On December 12, 1799, Washington developed pain after horseback riding in bad winter weather at Mount Vernon. His throat swelled and doctors began to bleed him (a common treatment at the time). Two days later he was dead from epiglottitis, a throat infection.

THE PHANTOM GENERAL OF GETTYSBURG

Did George Washington come back from the dead to help the Union army during the Civil War? Some claim he led them to victory. The Twentieth Maine Regiment was on its way to the Battle of Gettysburg when they got lost. According to reports, an eerie figure on a white horse appeared and guided them to position in time for them to stop a Confederate attack. So many soldiers saw Washington's ghost that the Secretary of War investigated. The regiment's commander, Colonel Joshua Chamberlain, testified, "We know not what mystic power may be possessed by those who are now bivouacking [living] with the dead . . . Who shall say that Washington was not among the number of those who aided the country that he founded?"

Here Washington rides Blueskin, one of two horses he rode during the Revolutionary War. The horse was said to be somewhat skittish in gunfire.

the Poison Pills of LEWIS & CLARK

Lewis and Clark relied on Sacagawea as an interpreter for the Native American tribes they encountered during their journey.

Before Meriwether Lewis set out with William Clark in 1804 to map and explore the territory acquired in the Louisiana Purchase, he studied medicine with Benjamin Rush, one of the country's leading physicians.

Rush put together a list of medical supplies for Lewis and Clark to take on their trip. Among them were hundreds of "Bilious Pills" that Rush created to rid the body of waste. Known as "Thunderclappers" for their

Benjamin Rush served as the Surgeon General of the Army during the Revolutionary War and was one of the signers of the Declaration of Independence.

Benjamin Rush

Mercurous chloride, Mild, Pills, Compound

COMPOUND MILD MERCUROUS CHLORIDE PILLS
Pilulæ Hydrargyri Chloridi Mitis Compositæ

Pil. Hydrarg. Chlorid. Mit. Comp.   Compound Cathartic Pills

Compound colocynth Extract	8 Gm.
Mild Mercurous Chloride	6 Gm.
Jalap Resin, in fine powder	2 Gm.
Gamboge, in very fine powder	1.5 Gm.
Diluted Alcohol, a sufficient quantity,	
To make 100 pills.	

Prepare the pills according to the General Directions, page 739.
AVERAGE DOSE—2 pills.

One average metric dose contains 0.16 Gm. of Compound Colocynth Extract, 0.12 Gm. of Mild Mercurous Chloride, 40 mg. of Jalap Resin, and 30 mg. of Gamboge.

effectiveness, they were composed of mercury chloride, a poison, and jalap, a powerful laxative. **The toxic pills, which were about four times the size of a typical aspirin pill, caused explosive pooping.** The explorers used them often, as their diet was mainly meat and very little fiber.

Considering that the pills were packed with deadly mercury, it is surprising how many men actually survived the eight-thousand-mile round-trip journey through the wilderness to the Pacific Ocean and back. Out of thirty-three men, only one died. He is thought to have suffered a burst appendix, from which not even a doctor in a hospital at that time could have saved him.

One of the ways historians and scientists have now traced the explorers' journey is by following the trail of mercury they left behind when they went to the bathroom!

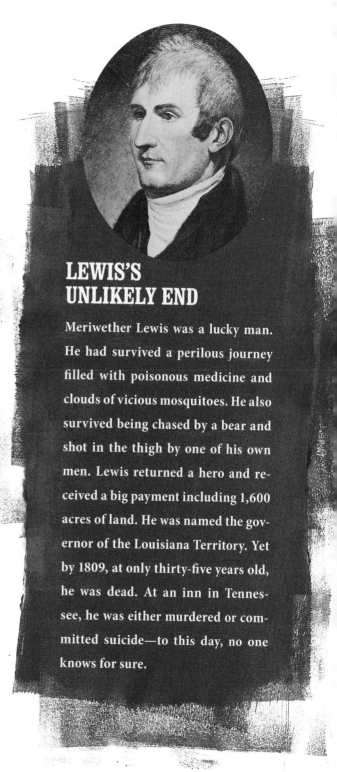

LEWIS'S UNLIKELY END

Meriwether Lewis was a lucky man. He had survived a perilous journey filled with poisonous medicine and clouds of vicious mosquitoes. He also survived being chased by a bear and shot in the thigh by one of his own men. Lewis returned a hero and received a big payment including 1,600 acres of land. He was named the governor of the Louisiana Territory. Yet by 1809, at only thirty-five years old, he was dead. At an inn in Tennessee, he was either murdered or committed suicide—to this day, no one knows for sure.

The Embarrassing Defeats AT LACOLLE

Major General Henry Dearborn fought with Benedict Arnold at the Battle of Quebec, where he was captured and held prisoner for a year.

Few battles in American history were as humiliating as those at the Lacolle River on November 20, 1812, and Lacolle Mills on March 30, 1814. Both were part of the United States' sorry attempt to conquer lower Canada, which

Americans thought would be easy. Former president Thomas Jefferson wrote in a letter that it was a "mere matter of marching." However, they underestimated the country's size, rough terrain, and horrid weather, as well as the battle-ready British troops.

Nearly five thousand American troops gathered to seize a guardhouse area on the road to Montreal in the Canadian province of Quebec that was defended by fewer than one hundred Canadian soldiers and their Indian allies. They felt ready. Major General Henry Dearborn wrote about his troops, **"Bravery and patriotism will supply any deficiency in military discipline and tactics, which time and experience will render perfect."** But this was not exactly the case.

First, a number of the state troops refused to cross the border into Canada. So a force of 650 soldiers, followed by 300 other state troops, advanced in the middle of the night. The Canadians fired and then retreated, causing confusion among the Americans. At one point **the Americans were so disorganized that they were shooting at each other.** Amid the darkness and chaos the Americans retreated, some soldiers abandoning their weapons in their haste to get away. The Canadians kept control of the guardhouse.

A year and a half later, in March 1814, American forces returned to Canada in the melting snow. More than four thousand soldiers, led by Major General James Wilkinson, were attacked by Canadian troops in a series of small battles. The goal was to slow the American advance on a mill occupied by about 180 British troops on the Lacolle River. This delay gave the Canadians the time they needed to get reinforcements, increasing their numbers to four hundred. Though outnumbered ten to one, they had the eighteen-inch-thick stone walls of the mill to protect them. Hours of American cannon bombardment caused little damage. The small Canadian force

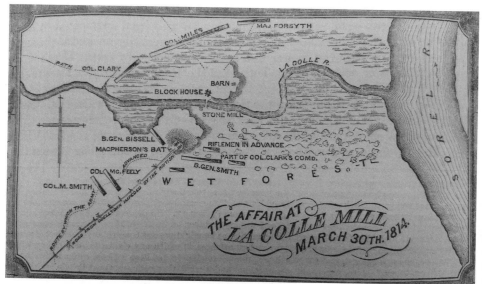

The American retreat at Lacolle was disorganized and embarrassing.

was able to hold off the attackers until darkness fell. With thirteen killed and fifty-one wounded, Wilkinson gave up and withdrew his American forces across the river, and the Canadians were triumphant once again.

WHO WON THE WAR OF 1812?

No one, really. The Treaty of Ghent, which was signed to end the war, basically stated that the borders of Canada and the United States were the same as they were before the war. The Canadians were pleased that they had stopped the American invasion, and the Americans were thrilled that they had beaten the British at the Battle of New Orleans—even though it occurred *after* the war was officially over. And the British? They were just happy to finally be able to go home.

Future president Andrew Jackson leading his troops to victory at the Battle of New Orleans.

Britain's Merciless Burning
OF WASHINGTON, D.C.

During the War of 1812, most of the early battles took place in the north, along the Canadian border. At the Raid on Port Dover in May 1814, American troops burned a number of private homes, in addition to mills and other important targets. In response

"British troops were required and directed to destroy and lay waste such towns and districts as you may find assailable."

Some say that is why the British targeted Washington, D.C. On August 24, 1814, 4,500 British troops advanced on the city. President

President Madison returned to Washington, D.C. three days after the British retreat. But he was never able to live in the White House again.

James Madison was at a battle in Bladensburg six miles outside of D.C., where the Americans were badly defeated. With the British on the move, he sent word to his wife, Dolley, to abandon the White

House just as she was laying out dinner for her husband's return. She gathered the most important papers and the silver, and asked for the Gilbert Stuart portrait of George Washington to be taken away. She escaped just as British soldiers entered the city.

Michael Shiner, a slave, saw the soldiers on Capitol Hill and recalled, **"As soon as we got sight of the British army raising that hill, they look like flames of fire, all red coats, and the stocks of their guns painted with red vermillion."**

British troops began setting fire to public buildings, including the Capitol and Supreme Court. Then they advanced on the White House.

There, as Captain Harry Smith later wrote, "We found a supper all ready, which was sufficiently cooked without more fire, and which many of us speedily consumed . . . and drank some very good wine also. I shall never forget the destructive majesty of the flames as the torches were

Dolley Madison didn't want to leave the White House until she knew her husband was safe. She wrote her sister, "We have had a battle or skirmish . . . and I am still here within sound of the cannon!"

applied to the beds, curtains, etc. Our sailors were artists at the work."

After twenty-six hours the destruction was complete. A huge storm blew over Washington, putting out many of the fires and forcing the British to retreat to their ships. While they were in the capital only a little more than a day, they inflicted damage that would take decades to repair.

BOOK BURNERS

In addition to destroying the most important buildings in Washington, D.C., the British also burned the three thousand books of the Library of Congress, which were then housed in the Capitol. Former president Thomas Jefferson, who had retired to his home, Monticello, offered to sell Congress his library, which was considered one of the finest in the world. For $23,950, the United States received 6,487 books on topics ranging from architecture and science to literature and geography. In 1886 a separate building was constructed to house the growing collection. The Library of Congress was the most expensive library ever built at the time and is still the largest library in the world today.

British soldier George Gleig later wrote that "a noble library, several printing presses, and all the national archives were likewise committed to the flames."

PART II: WESTERN EXPANSION AND REFORM (1829–1859)

1830 Underground Railroad established; Joseph Smith organizes the Mormon Church; U.S. population hits 12,860,702

1831 African American preacher Nat Turner leads a slave rebellion in Southampton County, Virginia

1831 The six-year campaign known as the Trail of Tears begins with the forced removal of Native Americans from their homes on the East Coast

1833 Andrew Jackson begins second term as president

1836 Texas declares independence from Mexico

1837 Martin Van Buren begins term as president

1837 Global economic crisis begins

1840 U.S. population hits 17,063,353

1841 Recently elected president William Henry Harrison dies of pneumonia after one month in office; he is succeeded by Vice President John Tyler

1845 James K. Polk begins term as president

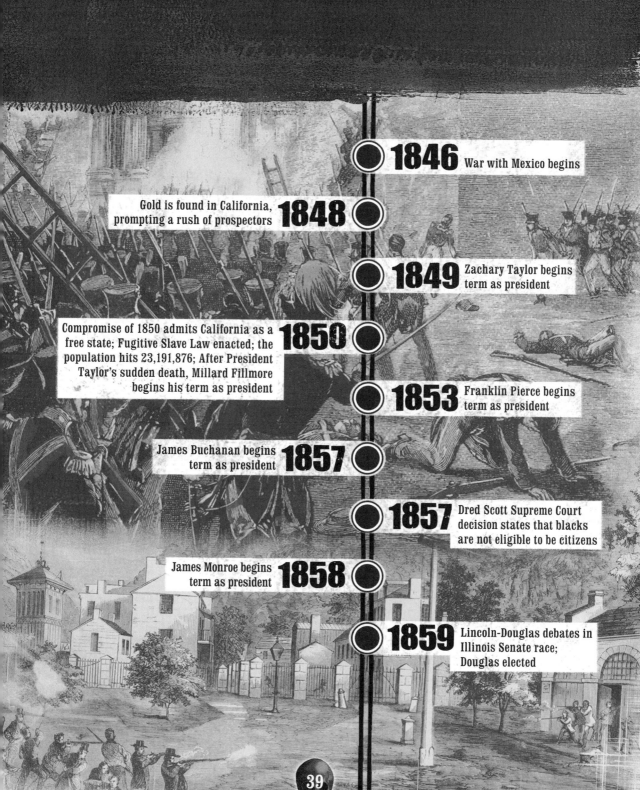

1846 War with Mexico begins

Gold is found in California, prompting a rush of prospectors **1848**

1849 Zachary Taylor begins term as president

Compromise of 1850 admits California as a free state; Fugitive Slave Law enacted; the population hits 23,191,876; After President Taylor's sudden death, Millard Fillmore begins his term as president **1850**

1853 Franklin Pierce begins term as president

James Buchanan begins term as president **1857**

1857 Dred Scott Supreme Court decision states that blacks are not eligible to be citizens

James Monroe begins term as president **1858**

1859 Lincoln-Douglas debates in Illinois Senate race; Douglas elected

ANDREW JACKSON: Too Mean to Die

Andrew Jackson never shirked from a fight. Even as a 13-year-old prisoner during the Revolutionary War, he refused to clean a British soldier's boots. In response, he was slashed across the face with a sword. Jackson would carry the scar for the rest of his life. He described his temperament as **"I was born for a storm, and a calm does not suit me."**

Andrew Jackson

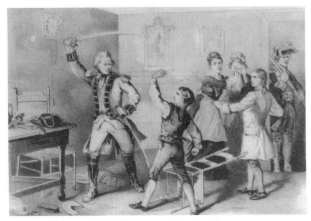

Along with being slashed by a sword during the war, Andrew Jackson lost his mother and brother to smallpox and his other brother to heatstroke.

A lifelong military man, he was known as "Old Hickory" because he was as tough and unyielding as the hard wood. He fought in a number of duels; survived smallpox; and battled Indians, who gave him the name "Sharp Knife." He famously said, **"I try to live my life as if death might come for me at any moment."**

On January 30, 1835, it arrived in the form of Richard Lawrence, a deranged house painter. Lawrence believed that the U.S. government owed him money and that Jackson was keeping it from him. Once Lawrence got the funds, he could return to England, where he believed he would be crowned king.

During the presidential election, Jackson's opponent circulated these coffin handbills, which detailed the soldiers put to death under Jackson's command during the War of 1812.

COLD-BLOODED KILLER

Before Jackson was president, he was a murderer. An argument over a horse race turned deadly when Jackson challenged Charles Dickinson, one of the best shots in Tennessee, to a duel. They met on May 30, 1806, in Kentucky, where dueling was legal. With pistols, they both took aim but Dickinson fired first, hitting Jackson in the chest and breaking two of his ribs. Per the rules of the duel, Dickinson now had to stand there while Jackson took his shot. Often in cases like this, the second shooter would purposefully aim away. Not Jackson. He aimed carefully and pulled the trigger, hitting Dickinson in a single shot that killed him. Then Jackson collapsed. The bullet in Jackson's chest was too close to his heart to remove safely, so it remained there the rest of his long life. The doctor who examined Jackson said, "I don't see how you stayed on your feet after that wound." Jackson responded, "I would have stood up long enough to kill him if he had put a bullet in my brain."

Approaching Jackson as he left the Capitol building, Lawrence raised his derringer but the gun misfired. A furious 67-year-old Jackson rushed his attacker, clubbing Lawrence several times with his walking cane while yelling, "Let me alone, let me alone." During the scuffle, Lawrence managed to pull out a second loaded pistol and pulled the trigger, but it also misfired. Onlookers, including frontiersman Davy Crockett, wrestled Lawrence away from the furious president.

For attempting to kill Jackson, Lawrence spent the rest of his life in a mental institution. Jackson died at 78 in his home, of sickness and old age.

The odds that both guns would misfire were later determined to be 125,000 to 1.

Victory or Death
AT THE ALAMO

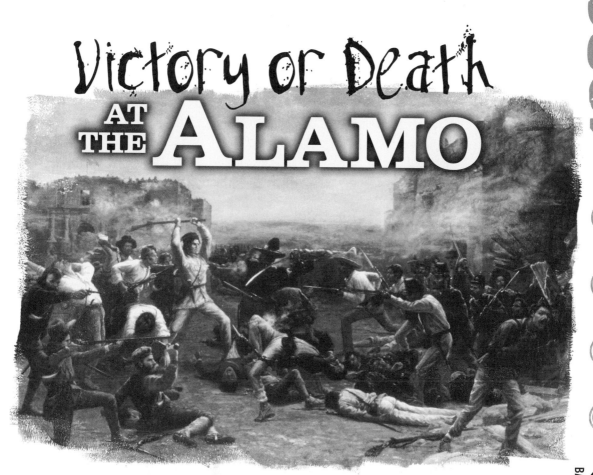

A townsperson wrote of the Texians' heroic last stand, "The gallantry of the . . . Texians . . . [was] really wondered at by the Mexican army. Even the generals were astonished at their vigorous resistance, and how dearly victory had been bought."

During the Texas war for independence from Mexico, Texas soldiers took over the Alamo—a mission, or religious outpost, near present-day San Antonio. On February 23, 1836, thousands of Mexican troops led by General Antonio López de Santa Anna surrounded the mission that a force of Texians, as they were then called, had turned into a fort. The two hundred defenders—commanded by pioneer James Bowie, soldier William Travis, and former frontiersman and congressman Davy Crockett—held them off for thirteen days. Travis wrote letters requesting aid and had them smuggled out. One read:

"FELLOW-CITIZENS AND COMPATRIOTS: I am besieged

by a thousand or more of the Mexicans under Santa Anna. I have sustained a continued bombardment for twenty-four hours, and have not lost a man. The enemy have demanded a surrender at discretion . . . I have answered the summons with a cannon-shot, and our flag still waves proudly from the walls. **I shall never surrender or retreat . . . Victory or death!**"

And death was a strong possibility. Santa Anna let the Texian soldiers know that if they fought, there would be no quarter. This meant they would not be taken prisoner if captured but would be killed. He raised a bloodred flag from a nearby church at the start of the siege so it would be clear to the Texians that none of their lives would be spared. Some also say that he had a bugler play the song "El Degüello," known as the "throat-cutting song," when the flag was raised. But still the Texians did not surrender.

On the thirteenth day Santa Anna

During the battle, the Mexican army charged twice and were "stopped by the deadly fire of Travis's artillery, which resembled a constant thunder."

attacked with all his might. The *Saturday Evening Post* reported: ". . . On the 6th March, about midnight, the Alamo was assaulted by the whole force of the Mexican army, commanded by [Gen. Antonio López de] Santa Anna in person. The battle was desperate until daylight, when only seven men belonging to the Texian Garrison were found alive, who cried for quarters, but were told that **there was no mercy for them—they then continued fighting until the whole were butchered**."

News of the massacre made Americans furious. Many rushed to join the Texian army. On April 21, 1836, commander Sam Houston led eight hundred troops in a surprise attack on Santa Anna's 1,600 men camped near present-day Houston. Shouting,

"Remember the Alamo!"

the Texian army attacked. The fighting was fierce but the battle was brief. After eighteen minutes, nearly seven hundred Mexican troops were dead, Santa Anna was captured, and the Mexicans surrendered. The war was over, and Texas secured its independence. It remained an independent republic for nearly ten years before becoming part of the United States in 1845.

SPIRITS OF THE SLAIN

After his victory at the Alamo, Santa Anna ordered the destruction of the mission-fort. However, when soldiers approached the building with flaming torches, six spirits were said to appear, frightening them off. It later served as a prison for the city of San Antonio. Newspaper stories between 1894 and 1897 reported prisoners' sightings of a ghostly sentry that was said to patrol the roof of the building. The prison was subsequently closed. Other people later claimed that they saw a figure dressed in buckskin clothing in various spots around the Alamo. Could it be the ghost of Davy Crockett, famed frontiersman thought to have died so violently there?

THE MANY WAYS TO BE KILLED ON THE OREGON TRAIL

Many died crossing rivers on the trail. Celinda Hines, whose family tried to cross the Snake River in 1853, was horrified as she watched her father drown.

Before the transcontinental railroad's first journey in 1869, the most common route for settlers going to California and points west was the 2,200-mile Oregon Trail. The five-month wagon trip was dangerous and often deadly. Of the two hundred thousand who made the trip during the nineteenth century, more than twenty thousand died. Many feared being attacked by Native Americans, because the trail passed through the lands of the Fox, Sauk, Potawatomi, Sioux, Shoshone, Nez Perce, Cayuse, and Shawnee tribes. Though there were some attacks, Indians were not nearly as great of a danger as the many other perils the travelers faced.

For example, the wagons themselves were so large and heavy they could squash you like a bug. Children or adults who slipped under the wheels while walking or getting out of the wagon could be killed. Edward Lenox, who was sixteen years old when his family emigrated in 1843, later wrote, **"A little boy fell over the front end of the wagon during our journey. In his case, the great wheels rolled over the child's head— crushing it to pieces."**

River crossings were also treacherous. The fifteen-foot wagons pulled by oxen could tip, drowning riders and losing supplies.

Fanny Kelly

KIDNAPPED ON THE TRAIL

While some settlers did die from Indian attacks on the trail, the sensational coverage of them in newspapers made it seem much more common. One of the most famous stories of that time was the kidnapping of nineteen-year-old Fanny Kelly by the Oglala Sioux in Wyoming in July 1864. In her autobiography she wrote, "Without a sound of preparation or a word of warning, the bluffs before us were covered with a party of about two hundred and fifty Indians, painted and equipped for war, who fired a signal volley of guns and revolvers in the air." Many in her wagon train were killed and she was captured.

She was held for five months, about which she wrote, "True, the Oglalas had treated me at times with great harshness and cruelty, yet I had never suffered from any of them the slightest personal or unchaste insult." She was finally ransomed at Fort Sully for three horses and a wagonload of supplies.

People crossing were swept away by the currents. Ferrymen sprung up along the banks of the Kansas, North Platte, Green, and Columbia Rivers, charging as much as they could to carry people across the raging waters.

Cholera was the most deadly disease on the Oregon Trail.

This bacterial infection of the small intestine, caused by drinking dirty water, can kill a person in a few hours. But settlers also died from diphtheria, dysentery, measles, and typhoid fever. John Clark wrote of his experience: "One woman and two men lay dead on the grass and some more ready to die. Women and children crying, some hunting medicine and none to be found. With heartfelt sorrow, we looked around for some time until I felt unwell myself. Got up and moved forward one mile, so as to be out of hearing of crying and suffering."

Indian attacks were not common on the trail and more Indians than settlers were thought to have been killed between 1840 and 1860.

Cannibalism
ON THE TRAIL TO CALIFORNIA

The 600-mile Sierra Nevada mountain range in California. Between October and May, the peaks can receive as much as 30 feet of snow.

In 1846 a caravan of eighty-seven pioneers known as the Donner Party attempted to use an untried route across the Sierra Nevada Mountains to California. This longer route meant they didn't reach the Sierra Nevadas until late October, when the dangerous winter snows started. A series of snowstorms trapped them in the mountains for five months. With few supplies their means of survival made them infamous. **In order not to starve to death, the surviving pioneers ate some of their dead.**

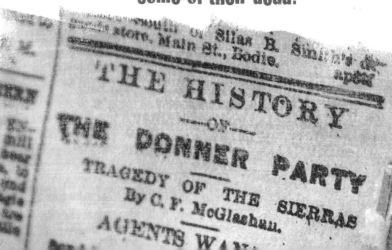

On December 27, 1846, Patrick Breen wrote, "snow nine feet deep; wood growing scarce." Two weeks later he wrote, "They have nothing but hides to live on."

made, for the many snowfalls of winter were banked about them firm as granite walls, and in that camp was neither implement nor arm strong enough to reach their resting places." However, one of the group's rescuers, Daniel Rhoads, wrote in a letter in 1847, **"We were seven days going to them. The people were dying every day. They had been living on dead bodies for weeks."**

Eliza Donner, the four-year-old daughter of group organizer George Donner, was one who survived. She later wrote in 1911 that the claims of cannibalism were false, and that they lived on hides. "The fact was, our dead could not have been disturbed even had the attempt been

Whatever the truth, they weren't the only ones accused of resorting to cannibalism at that time. Alferd Packer and a group of prospectors left Provo, Utah, in February 1874 for Breckenridge, Colorado, in search of gold. Trapped in a blizzard in the Rocky Mountains, Packer reached Breckenridge in April, the only one still alive. In his possession were money and a rifle belonging to the others in the group. Packer's first confession claimed that the group

"Dolly" made the trip over the mountains in the pocket of eight-year-old Donner Party survivor Patty Reed.

THE LEGEND OF LIVER-EATING JOHNSTON

Born John Garrison, Johnston changed his last name after he left the U.S. Navy over a fight with an officer. He moved to the mountains of Montana and Wyoming, where he made a living as a whiskey trader and fur trapper, and by cutting firewood for steamships on the Missouri River. Johnston became infamous for a story that few are sure is true. One day when Johnston was out hunting in 1847, a party of Crow Indians killed his wife, an Indian woman who was supposedly pregnant at the time. The angry Johnston swore revenge and waged a one-man war against the Crow. After each time he killed someone, he was said to cut out the dead man's liver and eat it. Johnston later said it was an exaggeration of what truly happened, but the legend lives on.

Johnston wrote that he cut out the liver of a Sioux Indian and asked a friend if he wanted a bit. "He refused but told everyone he seen me eating the Indian liver," which was where he got the nickname.

became trapped and, as men died from starvation and "accidents," the others eventually ate them. He was jailed until authorities could learn more.

In August a search party found the bones of the five men. They had been bound, hacked to death, and cannibalized, proof that Packer's statement was a lie. When the search party returned to confront Packer, they found that he had escaped jail.

Almost nine years later he was recaptured and put on trial. In a new confession Packer claimed that while

A traveling illustrator for Harper's Weekly *drew the five dead and butchered men, who had been rotting for months when found.*

he was out hunting, one of his party, Shannon Bell, went mad with hunger and killed the other four. Packer returned to find Bell alone, roasting one of their companion's legs over a fire. Bell attacked him as well, so Packer shot him in self-defense. Unable to escape in the snow, Packer lived off the flesh of the men Bell had killed.

Packer's trial began in 1883. During his two hours on the stand, he lied a number of times in obvious ways, even about simple things, such as his age. The jury found him guilty and he was sentenced to hanging. However, two years later, Packer won the right to a new trial due to the fact that Colorado was a territory, not a state, when the murder was committed. In this trial he was sentenced to forty years in jail, and he served less than half of the time.

Olive Oatman's Kidnapping
AND LIFE
WITH
THE
MOHAVE

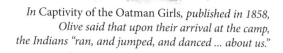

In Captivity of the Oatman Girls, *published in 1858, Olive said that upon their arrival at the camp, the Indians "ran, and jumped, and danced ... about us."*

In 1851 Olive Oatman's Mormon pioneer family, traveling through northern Arizona Territory, was heading west to create a settlement in California. Separated from the rest of their wagon train, they were set upon by a band of Yavapai Indians, who killed most of the family. Olive, orphaned at thirteen, and her younger sister Mary Ann lived with the tribe for a year.

An 1856 newspaper article in the *Los Angeles Star* described the sisters' acceptance into Mohave society: "Arrived among the Mohaves, **the Chief, whom she calls *Espanesay*, took them into his own family, and they were treated in every respect as his own children.**

Two blankets were given to them for covering; food was divided with them; they were not obliged to labor, but did pretty much as they pleased . . . The Mohaves always told [Olive] she could go to the white settlement when she pleased, but

Olive Oatman, pictured here with the Mohave tattoos on her chin.

way of identifying people in the afterlife. Olive would later write, "We had seen them do this to some of their female children, and we had often conversed with each other about expressing the hope that we should be spared from receiving their marks upon us. **I ventured to plead with them for a few moments that they would not put those ugly marks upon our faces. But it was in vain . . .** They told us this could never be taken from the face . . . and that they could claim us in whatever tribe they might find us." Soon after, during a drought, Mary Ann, along with many Mohave, died of starvation.

they dared not go with her, fearing they might be punished for having kept a white woman so long among them." The sisters didn't know where the white settlement was located, though, so they never tried to escape.

Olive and Mary Ann were both marked with blue tattoos on their chins, like all Mohave women. The Indians believed that tattoos were a

In 1856 Lieutenant Martin Burke at Fort Yuma in California near the Arizona border heard about Olive through travelers. He sent an Indian named Francisco to barter with the Mohave for Olive's return. The chief finally agreed to let her go for beads, two horses, and two blankets. At age nineteen, she was successfully brought back to Fort Yuma.

Olive was reunited with her one remaining brother, and she teamed up with a pastor to write her memoirs, later traveling on a nationwide speaking tour. After marrying and moving to Texas, she lived into her sixties, finally dying of a heart attack.

TRYING TO WIPE OUT INDIAN CULTURE, ONE STUDENT AT A TIME

White children weren't the only ones taken from their families and forced to live in a culture strange and different from their own. Many Indian children were sent to boarding schools, where they were forced to live like white people. In 1879 Richard Henry Pratt founded the United States Indian Industrial School in Carlisle, Pennsylvania. Pratt's motto was: "Kill the Indian, Save the Man." Students were given short haircuts, uniforms, and new English names. They were not allowed to speak their languages, even to each other, or engage in any native customs. The school was run like the military, with strict discipline. Children didn't go home for years at a time. In the thirty-nine years it was open, more than ten thousand Native American children went to Carlisle. The growth of schools on Indian reservations helped bring an end to the despicable program.

Native American students at the Carlisle Indian School in 1884.

BATTLE

THE MOUNTAIN MEADOWS
Massacre

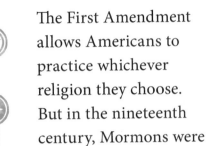

The First Amendment allows Americans to practice whichever religion they choose. But in the nineteenth century, Mormons were discriminated against. Members moved westward in search of a "promised land" where they could worship the way they wanted to in peace. In 1847 Mormons arrived in the remote territory of Utah. However, non-Mormons still traveled through their lands, which caused conflict.

An 1882 political cartoon warns European immigrants about the danger awaiting them in Utah.

On September 7, 1857, in a mountain valley three hundred miles south of Salt Lake City, a group of Mormons and local Indians attacked the Fancher party, a wagon train of Arkansas families bound for California. The pioneers held the attackers off for five days but were running out of water and ammunition. So when the Mormons approached the families to surrender under a flag of truce and a pledge of safe passage, the Fancher party felt they had to accept. They were led away, with women and children in the front. Men were in the rear, each with a Mormon bodyguard.

After walking for a while, the call was made: "Do your duty!" Suddenly the air was filled with the sound of gunfire.

In the space of five minutes, 120 men, women, and children were murdered. Only seventeen children under eight years old, considered the age of innocence in the Mormon faith, were allowed to live. The bodies of those slaughtered were stripped of clothes and jewelry and left to rot, and the young survivors were taken in by Mormon families.

Why was the wagon train of people murdered? One of the reasons was timing—the party left Arkansas in the spring of 1857, just as Mormons in the Utah Territory and the United States were on the brink of war. Also, Mormon zealots believed they were doing God's work by ridding the world of nonbelievers and that murder in defense of faith was just. And finally, the Fancher wagon train, with its large supply of cash and weapons and hundreds of valuable horses and cattle, was too big of a temptation for the poor Mormon settlers to let pass.

In the August 13, 1859, issue of *Harper's Weekly*, Brevet Major Carleton described the killing

A drawing from an 1877 Frank Leslie's Illustrated Newspaper, *showing the execution of Mormon John D. Lee.*

field two years later as "one too horrible and sickening for language to describe. Human skeletons, disjointed bones, ghastly skulls, and the hair of women were scattered in frightful profusion over a distance of two miles . . . **the remains were not buried at all until after they had been dismembered by the wolves and the flesh stripped from the bones,** and then only such bones were buried as lay scattered along nearest the road." Carleton gathered the bones and buried them in a single grave.

In 1858 Mormon leader Brigham Young claimed that local Paiute Indians were responsible. However, once it became clear that Mormons were involved, he placed blame for the killings on extremist John D. Lee, although in reality more than fifty men were involved. Nearly two decades and two trials passed before Lee was convicted. His punishment? Execution by firing squad in 1877.

HOW THE SEAGULL SAVED SALT LAKE CITY

In May 1848 hordes of crickets attacked the Mormon settlers' crops. Orson F. Whitney, an apostle, or officer, of the Mormon faith, later wrote, "When it seemed that nothing could stay the devastation, great flocks of gulls appeared, filling the air with their white wings and plaintive cries, and settled down upon the half-ruined fields. All day long they gorged themselves, and when full, disgorged and feasted again, the white gulls upon the black crickets." By eating and driving off the crickets, the gull became beloved in Utah. It is now the state bird. There is even a statue in Salt Lake City, pictured below, commemorating the event known as "The Miracle of the Gulls."

John Brown, Harper's Ferry, AND THE Failed Slave Revolt

John Brown's fighters were trapped when state troops began firing on them.

Slavery had existed in the United States since colonial times. Over the years the question of whether to continue the horrible practice divided the North and South. People in the North who wanted to abolish slavery were called abolitionists. In the 1850s John Brown, a white man, was the most famous and

John Brown

dangerous abolitionist in the country because he was known to kill slave owners and sympathizers. He also wanted to help slaves revolt.

In October 1859 Brown tried to make this dream a reality. He and his men raided the U.S. Arsenal at Harper's Ferry, Virginia.

EN ROUTE FOR HARPER'S FERRY.—[Sketched by Porte Crayon.]

John Brown's men on the way to Harper's Ferry, as Brown said he was "now quite certain that the crimes of this guilty land will never be purged away but with blood."

Their goal? To capture its armory, where one hundred thousand guns were stored, and give the weapons to slaves to launch a rebellion.

The small band of abolitionists snuck into town and cut the telegraph wires. One member of Brown's group, African American Osborne Perry Anderson, helped liberate nearby slaves and capture slaveholders as hostages.

The hostages included Lewis W. Washington, the great-grandnephew of President George Washington. Anderson later wrote, "The first prisoner taken by us was Lewis Washington . . . The Colonel cried heartily when he found he must submit, and appeared taken aback when, upon delivering up the famous sword formerly presented by Frederic [the Great of Prussia] to his illustrious kinsman, George Washington, Capt.

Stevens told me to step forward and take it . . . [Me] being a colored man, and colored men being only things in the South, it is proper that the South be taught a lesson upon this point."

While the raid was successful in the sense that the armory was captured, the slave uprising Brown had predicted did not happen. The fighters took shelter in the armory's engine house and exchanged fire with the local militia, or state troops. Lewis Washington later wrote that John Brown "was the coolest and firmest man I ever saw in defying danger and death."

SLAVE INSURRECTION OF 1811

While John Brown's slave rebellion never happened, one did occur in January 1811 in the territory that later became Louisiana. Armed mostly with hand tools, between two hundred and five hundred enslaved men escaped at night and began a two-day, twenty-mile march toward New Orleans. Along the way they burned five plantation houses and killed two men. A militia quickly gathered to fight the mob. After a brief battle, approximately forty slaves were killed and the rest scattered into the swamps, where they were difficult to follow. One of the slave leaders, Charles Deslondes, was captured a few days later. Samuel Hambleton, a naval agent in New Orleans, wrote that Deslondes had his "hands chopped off then shot in one thigh and then the other, until they were both broken."

Another twenty-nine men were found and executed, and many of their heads were put on pikes as a warning to other slaves who were considering rebelling.

The fighters were holed up in the engine house of the Harper's Ferry Armory until troops rammed the door.

John Brown leaving the jail on the morning of his execution.

The next day Anderson witnessed John Brown's capture by the U.S. Marines under Colonel Robert E. Lee: "The old hero and his men were hacked and wounded with indecent rage, and at last brought out of the house and laid prostrate upon the ground, mangled and bleeding as they were . . . Wiser and better men no doubt there were, but a braver man [than John Brown] never lived." Robert E. Lee had less respect for Brown, as he wrote in his report:

"The result proves that the plan was the attempt of a fanatic or madman, which could only end in failure."

After his capture, when asked upon what principle he justified his acts, Brown replied: **"Upon the golden rule. I pity the poor in bondage [slavery] that have none to help them; that is why I am here . . . It is my sympathy with the oppressed and the wronged, that are as good as you and as precious in the sight of God."** Brown was put on trial and was found guilty of treason, murder, and "conspiring with Negroes to produce insurrection." He was executed by hanging on December 2, 1859.

PART III: CIVIL WAR AND RECONSTRUCTION (1860–1869)

1860 South Carolina secedes from the Union

Abraham Lincoln begins term as president; eleven pro-slavery Southern states secede from the Union; Jefferson Davis elected president of the Confederacy; Civil War begins **1861**

1863 Emancipation Proclamation issued, freeing slaves in the Confederate states

Civil War ends with the Confederacy's surrender; President Lincoln is assassinated; Thirteenth Amendment to the Constitution is ratified, ending slavery **1865**

THE PACKED PEMBERTON MILL,
A Recipe for Death

More than 100 died in ruins of the Pemberton Mill and the ensuing fire. The Boston Globe *wrote that some were "burned to death in the sight of their loved ones, who were powerless to aid them."*

The Pemberton Mill, a cotton factory in Lawrence, Massachusetts, was 280 feet long and five stories tall, and employed nearly eight hundred workers who labored at seven hundred looms. The building was poorly constructed, and the mill's owners had packed it with so many heavy looms and other machinery that working conditions were dangerous. On January 10, 1860,

disaster struck when the outer walls began to buckle.

The *Boston Journal* reported that, just before five p.m. that day, "without the slightest note of warning, the ceiling of the upper floor separated from the walls on either side, and in another instant carried each floor, with burdens of machinery, iron, and timbers, to the bottom, where, with 600 people, a pyramid was formed, rising over

50 feet. The wall, thus freed from the internal support . . . completed the wreck. **The moans and cries for help of those in the ruins whose lives had not been immediately crushed out, mingled with an alarm rung out by the factory bells, called almost the entire community to the spot."**

The *New York Times* reported, "Mr. A. B. Winne was in the fifth story when he felt the shaking of the building. He expected to be instantly killed, but went down with the falling mass to the first floor, and walked out of the ruins unharmed. He was obliged to tear away some timbers

COULDN'T WAIT FOR DEATH

Vincent's Semi-Annual United States Register, a publication that every six months produced a record of the significant events in the nation, reported, "Perhaps one of the saddest episodes of the whole calamity was the fate of Mr. Maurice Palmer, who was an overseer in the mill. In the fall, he was so embedded in the ruins that he could not be extricated [pulled out] before the fire; and, seeing the dreadful element approaching him, he, in his agony and despair, determined not to be roasted to death, and so drew his pocketknife and cut his throat. He was, however, taken out alive, and would have survived but for the self-inflicted injury."

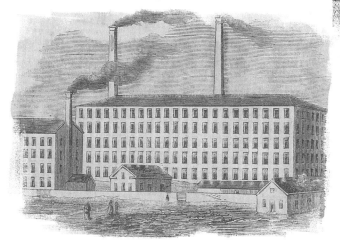

Pemberton Mill before the collapse and fire.

to get out . . . the wounded and imprisoned in the vicinity beseeching him not to move anything for fear the rubbish would crush them."

The wintry darkness made the scene even more terrible. While thousands came to help, no one could see the injured.

"One of them thrust her arm through the small aperture, and begged to be drawn through but before the hole could be enlarged, the poor girl and her fellow prisoners perished in the flames."

Even with the challenges, more than two hundred people were rescued from under the beams and iron pillars. Yet the oil lamps that lit the way were their ultimate undoing. That night two men carried in lanterns to help find a young woman, and one of the lamps broke. **The lantern's hot oil caught fire on the factory's cotton, and in a few hours the rest of the debris and remaining trapped people were consumed in the flames.**

More than 120 people were killed and 160 were wounded, though some estimates are higher. The Pemberton Mill collapse is considered one of the worst industrial calamities in American history.

Worked to Death
ALONG THE TRANSCONTINENTAL RAILROAD

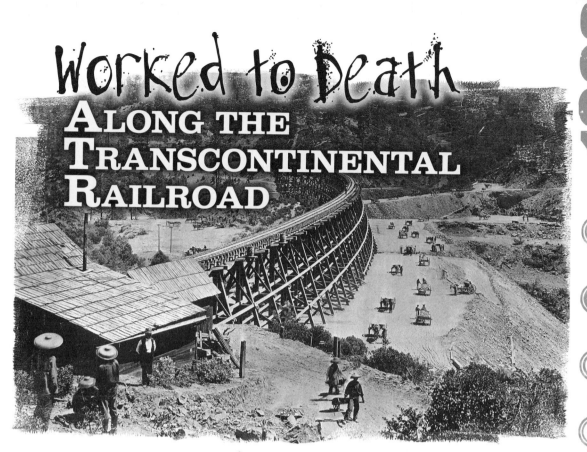

Chinese workers in 1868 next to the Central Pacific's Secret Town Trestle, which was 1,100 feet long, and 90 feet high, and was constructed over the divide between the American River and the Bear River.

Ever since pioneers began settling the West Coast, the public dreamed of a transcontinental railroad that would cross the wilderness and unite the nation. The federal government gave two railroad companies permission to build the railroad. The Union Pacific Railroad Company, starting at Council Bluffs, Iowa, would go west. The Central Pacific Railroad Company, starting at Sacramento, California, would go east. At some point they would meet.

In 1863 the Central Pacific Railroad Company began construction. But finding workers to build the transcontinental railroad was difficult. The first Chinese laborers were hired in 1865, though many white laborers were upset that the railroad was hiring foreigners.

PROGRESS

By 1868, eighty percent of the workers, nearly twelve thousand men, were Chinese. The rest of the workers were mainly Irish immigrants. Working in groups of thirty under a white foreman, the Chinese were paid an average of thirty dollars a month, which was less than their Irish counterparts. They worked from dawn to dusk six days a week and lived in camps along the tracks, where they cooked their own food. **Because most of the Central Pacific's route was mountainous, work was done at dizzying heights and on dangerous rocky slopes.**

During the summer of 1867, construction reached the Sierra Nevada Mountains at an elevation of seven thousand feet. One day the Chinese laborers abruptly stopped working and went back to camp. Before they would return, they had a few reasonable demands: They wanted to be paid

Chinese Central Pacific construction crews along the Humboldt Plains in Nevada.

forty dollars a month, to work only ten hours a day, and to have shorter shifts in the tunnels. **Management refused and simply cut off supplies to the laborers.** After a week without food, they were told they had to return to work or they would be fined a month's wages. Most returned, with no change to their situation.

On April 28, 1869, railroad management challenged the Chinese crews to lay ten miles of track in a single

The joining of the rails ceremony, which included driving the final gold spike, excluded the Chinese workers.

day. Together with eight Irish rail handlers, they laid ten miles and fifty-six feet of new track, spiking 3,520 rail lengths to 25,800 wooden ties. On May 10, 1869, the Chinese helped lay the last rail that joined the Central Pacific Railroad with the Union Pacific to complete the transcontinental line at Promontory Summit, Utah. However, no Chinese workers appear in the celebratory photo of that day (shown at left).

TRACKS OF DEATH

How many Chinese died building the railroad? One estimate is 137 workers, which seems very low considering the number of total workers and the dangerous nature of the work. In 1870 a journalist for the *Sacramento Reporter* set the number much higher, writing, "The accumulated bones of perhaps 1,200 Chinamen came in by the eastern train yesterday from along the line of the Central Pacific Railroad. The lot comprises [is made up of] about 20,000 pounds. Nearly all of them are the remains of employees of the company, who were engaged in building the railroad." The bones were shipped back to China to be buried.

On the railroad between Omaha and Sacramento, there were nineteen tunnels, mostly near the summit of the mountains. In the winter, workers burrowed under the snow from their camps to the work sites, but it didn't keep them safe from avalanches, which killed dozens at a time.

The Ghosts OF GETTYSBURG

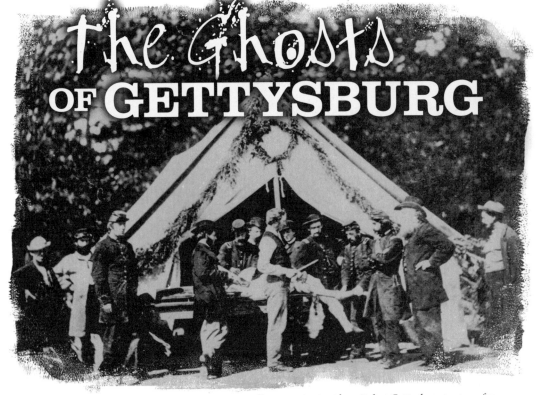

Doctors at a tent hospital at Gettysburg prepare for an amputation, one of many performed during the battle.

For three days in July 1863, more than 150,000 Union and Confederate soldiers clashed in Gettysburg, Pennsylvania. It was one of the bloodiest battles ever, with more than fifty thousand killed, wounded, or missing.

After the battle, nearly two thousand Union and three thousand Confederate wounded soldiers were too hurt to be sent to military hospitals. On July 22, 1863, more than four hundred tents from Camp Letterman Hospital were set up on the battlefield to care for them. **"Shrieks, cries, and groans resounded on all sides," one nurse wrote.** "Not only from those in the tents, but on the amputating tables, which were almost constantly occupied." Terrible injuries and infections took their toll, and soon more than 1,200 were buried in the camp cemetery.

Corporal Michael Dunn of the Pennsylvania Infantry Regiment, after the amputation of his legs in 1864.

each bare and dust-trampled space marking where corpses had lain after death-agony was passed, and where the wounded had groaned in pain. **Tears filled my eyes when I looked on that great field."**

Today, Gettysburg is considered one of the most haunted places in America. **The ghosts of the many soldiers who failed to survive have often been spotted on the former battlefield.** One—a young, legless man—appears to guests at a motel that was built over a site of heavy fighting.

The hospital finally closed on November 20, 1863. A nurse at the camp, Sophronia E. Bucklin, wrote, "The hospital tents were removed—

THREE-MINUTE AMPUTATIONS

At the time of the Civil War, doctors did not understand how infection spread, so a simple wound could end up killing a soldier. On the battlefield, surgeons often had little time to treat injuries, and amputations were common. Approximately thirty thousand were performed during the war. Surgeons would work around the clock on the battlefield. The average amputation on the field, performed with dull surgical knives, took about twelve minutes. A simple surgery of cutting off the leg at the knee could take only three minutes. By the end of a day, stacks of amputated limbs could be five feet high. The poet Walt Whitman saw it firsthand when visiting a battlefield in search of his brother, writing, "One of the first things that met my eyes in camp was a heap of feet, arms, legs, etc., under a tree in front of a hospital."

The Ugly Civil War Draft Riots IN NEW YORK CITY

During the draft riots, unruly mobs attacked storefronts and anyone unlucky enough to cross their path.

Ten days after the Union victory at Gettysburg, the people of New York City exploded in fury. On the morning of July 13, 1863, hundreds of men took to the streets to protest the federal draft lottery. All men between the ages of twenty and thirty-five, and all unmarried men between thirty-five and forty-five, were entered into a lottery where they could be drafted for military service.

Some New York City residents weren't completely behind the war, and many were angry that wealthy men could buy their way out of serving by paying someone $300 to take their place. **What started as a protest turned into a violent riot.** Military and government buildings were set ablaze. Since slavery was one reason for the war, the rioters turned their anger toward black people. They set fire to the Colored Orphan Asylum, home to 233 children. They hanged and burned a black man named William Jones and, over the course of the riot, beat to death or lynched ten others.

The violent chaos continued for four more days. Any black person who went outside would be chased by the mob. J. T. Headley wrote in *The Great Riots of New York*, "Sometimes a stalwart negro would break away from his murderers, and run for his life. With no place of safety to which he could flee, he would be headed off in every direction, and forced towards

the river. Driven at last to the end of a pier, he would leap off, preferring to take his chances in the water rather than among these bloody men."

Finally, on July 16, about four thousand federal troops marched into Manhattan from Gettysburg. They occupied the city and shot into the huge crowds that had been throwing

During the riots, crowds set fire to buildings and looted stores. The property damage totaled $1,500,000.

bricks and rocks at the police and soldiers. Headley wrote,

"Men and women reeled and fell on the sidewalk and in the street. One woman, with her child in her arms, fell, pierced with a bullet . . . [The crowd] seemed to think it hardly possible that the troops would fire point-blank into their midst. But the deadly effect of the fire convinced them of their error, and they began to jostle and crowd each other in the effort to get out of its range. **In a few minutes the avenue was cleared of the living, when the wounded and dead were cared for by their friends."** While the official death count was 119, many believe it was as high as one thousand people, as well as millions of dollars in property damage.

THE PRATT STREET RIOT OF 1861

The Civil War began on April 12, 1861, with the first shots fired at Fort Sumter, South Carolina. People in some states were divided on which side they supported. One week later the Washington Brigade of Pennsylvania Volunteers and the Sixth Massachusetts Militia traveled through Baltimore on their way to defend Washington, D.C. Baltimore was especially divided, with many Southern sympathizers. But it was a center for railroad transportation and anyone going to Washington, D.C. had to pass through it. Once the troops reached Baltimore they had to exit their train, march through the city, and board another train. Before they arrived, the unit's commander told the troops, "You will undoubtedly be insulted, abused, and, perhaps, assaulted, to which you must pay no attention whatever, but march with your faces to the front, and pay no attention to the mob, even if they throw stones, bricks, or other missiles; but if you are fired upon and any one of you is hit, your officers will order you to fire." They were attacked with stones, bricks, and pistols, and returned with gunfire. Four Union soldiers and approximately twelve civilians were killed as well as countless wounded.

Starving Mothers Riot for Bread IN RICHMOND

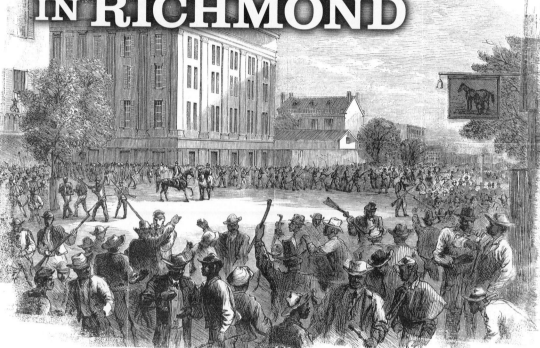

The women took to the streets of Richmond, demanding "bread or blood."

By 1863 Richmond, Virginia, was starving. Trade routes cut off by the Union army, combined with unusually heavy snowfalls, made getting food difficult and very expensive. To make matters worse Confederate president Jefferson Davis asked the hungry citizens to spend a day fasting and in prayer. As they already had no food to eat, the request just made people angrier.

On April 2 a group of poor working women marched to the capital to meet with the governor about the lack of food. He refused to meet with them, so the crowd took to the streets.

Union colonel Charles Stewart was a prisoner in Richmond at the time. He told the *New York Times* that "he saw from his prison window in Richmond a great bread riot, in which about three thousand women were engaged, armed with clubs, guns, and stones. They broke open the government stores and took bread, clothing, and whatever else they wanted. The militia were ordered out to check the riot, but failed to do so." **Shouting "bread or blood," they used axes to loot stores and break into warehouses.**

Jefferson Davis later recalled the day in a letter to the *Richmond Dispatch*, that he "made a brief address to the formidable crowd of both sexes, urging them to abstain from their lawless acts . . ."

A Richmond woman wrote in 1863 about a meeting with a bone-thin mother at the beginning of the riot, who said, "We are starving. As soon as enough of us get together, we are going to the bakeries and each of us will take a loaf of bread. That is little enough for the government to give us after it has taken all our men."

He concluded by saying:

"You say you are hungry and have no money. Here is all I have; it is not much, but take it."

He then, emptying his pockets, threw all the money they contained among the mob, after which he took out his watch and said: "We do not desire to injure anyone, but this lawlessness must stop. I will give you five minutes to disperse, otherwise you will be fired on."

Threatened with violence, the crowd trickled away. The next day officials set up guns around town. As many as seventy men and women received jail time for the riot, but most were released when officials realized they could not afford to feed the prisoners!

GLOW-IN-THE-DARK WOUNDS AT THE BATTLE OF SHILOH

During the Battle of Shiloh in April 1862, more than sixteen thousand soldiers were wounded. The huge number of injuries meant that many men had to lie in the mud for two rainy days, waiting for help from the overworked medics. Lying there, some noticed their wounds began to glow. Those that glowed seemed to heal faster than those that didn't. No one understood what was happening, so they called it "Angel's Glow." The mystery wasn't solved until 2001, when two high school students figured out that a good bacteria, *Panellus stipticus*—transported to the wounds of the cold soldiers by insects—caused the glow. The good bacteria fought the bad bacteria, which was trying to infect the wounds.

ANDERSONVILLE PRISON:
"Can This Be Hell?"

After spending months in Andersonville, strong soldiers were reduced to sick scarecrows.

Enemy troops captured in battle are called prisoners of war, or POWs. During the American Civil War, both the Union North and Confederate South had POW camps for the troops they captured. Some camps were tolerable, but many were awful. The worst POW camp in the Confederacy was in Georgia, near the town of Andersonville.

Robert H. Kellogg, a prisoner from the Sixteenth Regiment Connecticut Volunteers, wrote in his diary on May 2, 1864,

"As we entered [Andersonville Prison], a spectacle met our eyes that almost froze our blood with horror, and made our hearts fail within us.

BATTLE

Before us were forms that had once been active and erect—stalwart men, now nothing but mere walking skeletons, covered with filth and vermin. **Many of our men, in the heat and intensity of their feeling, exclaimed with earnestness, 'Can this be hell?'"**

Andersonville prison was built for ten thousand Union prisoners but as many as thirty thousand were housed there at its most crowded. During the war, more than forty-five thousand prisoners passed through the twenty-six-acre camp in fourteen months, making it by 1864 the fifth largest city by population in the Confederacy.

Kellogg continues, "In the center of the whole was a swamp, occupying about three or four acres of the narrowed limits, and a part of this marshy place had been used by the prisoners as a sink, and excrement covered the ground, the scent arising from which was suffocating."

As bad as conditions were in the beginning, near the end of the war, with the South losing and struggling to supply its own troops, things only got worse for the Union prisoners at Andersonville. More than thirteen thousand prisoners, nearly naked, with little shelter and almost no way to get clean water or food, died from disease and starvation.

"There is so much filth about the camp that it is terrible trying to live here.

New prisoners are made sick the first hours of their arrival by the stench which pervades the prison. Everybody's sick, almost, with scurvy—an awful disease," wrote prisoner John Ransom in his diary in 1864. "With sunken eyes, blackened countenances . . . the men look sickening. The air reeks with nastiness."

One way the Confederate guards kept so many prisoners from attempting to escape was the use of a dead line, which was an area next to the sixteen-foot-high fence that surrounded the camp. If a prisoner crossed the line, he was immediately shot. Private Samuel Elliot wrote, "A poor cripple shot for stepping inside the dead line; he said he was so miserable he wished to die, and took this means of having his wish gratified."

SOMEONE HAD TO PAY

Captain Henry Wirz ran the Andersonville prison for a year. He was known by the prisoners for his cruelty and rages. After the war he was charged and found guilty of working with Confederate officials to "impair and injure the health and destroy the lives . . . of Federal prisoners" so they wouldn't be strong enough to fight when they were released. However, much of what happened at Andersonville was not in his control. Wirz had been given few supplies and the Union refused to exchange prisoners, which led to overcrowding. Before his execution, Wirz told a reporter for the *Evening Star*, "As far as I am concerned, I have no hope of reprieve. These things which were done, somebody must suffer for. I have never denied that prisoners were mistreated; but it was not my fault. If I am the last one that is to suffer death for the Southern Confederacy, I am satisfied. I do not fear death." Wirz was hanged in Washington, D.C., on November 10, 1865, the only Confederate soldier convicted of war crimes.

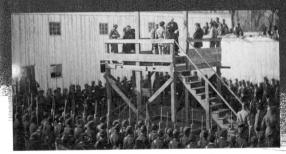

Captain Henry Wirz was hanged on November 10, 1865, at the Old Capitol Prison in Washington, D.C.

Lincoln Under Fire

AT FORT STEVENS

"Get down, you damn fool!" is not what

future Supreme Court justice Oliver Wendell Holmes Jr. had planned to say to President Abraham Lincoln. Yet he had also not expected that Lincoln would allow himself to be such an obvious six-foot-four-inch target for Confederate sharpshooters.

On July 11, 1864, Confederate lieutenant general Jubal Early's troops were in sight of the Capitol. The only thing between them and the city were forts manned by inexperienced troops.

Lincoln wasn't afraid of battle and once said, "The commander-in-chief of the army must not show any cowardice in the presence of his soldiers, whatever he may feel."

But a long march in the intense heat played a large part in stopping them from attacking that day.

President and Mrs. Lincoln rode out to Fort Stevens to observe the attack. General Horatio Wright asked somewhat jokingly if Lincoln would like to see the fight. Eager to witness combat, the president climbed to the top of the protective wall, seemingly oblivious to the bullets whizzing by. Only when a nearby surgeon was shot in the leg was General Wright able to convince Lincoln to take cover.

The arrival of Union reinforcements on July 12 prevented Early and the Confederates from continuing the attack. He withdrew that night but told one of his officers after the battle,

"We didn't take Washington but we scared Abe Lincoln like hell."

THE BULLET THAT DID KILL LINCOLN

While Lincoln avoided Confederate sharpshooters, he could not avoid the gun of assassin John Wilkes Booth on April 14, 1865. At 12:10 p.m. on the day after his death, an autopsy of President Lincoln took place in the White House. Assistant Surgeon Edward Curtis wrote to his mother that, during the autopsy, he and the other surgeon were attempting to find the bullet in Lincoln's skull. "Not finding it readily, we proceeded to remove the entire brain, when, as I was lifting the latter from the cavity of the skull, suddenly the bullet dropped out through my fingers and fell, breaking the solemn silence of the room with its clatter, into an empty basin that was standing beneath. There it lay upon the white china, a little black mass no bigger than the end of my finger—dull, motionless and harmless, yet the cause of such mighty changes in the world's history as we may perhaps never realize."

After shooting Lincoln, John Wilkes Booth shouted, "The South is avenged." He then jumped onto the stage and fled on horseback. Troops caught up with him and, when he wouldn't surrender, shot and killed him.

ABRAHAM LINCOLN'S
funeral train

Engine "Nashville" of the Lincoln funeral train, which pulled the train from Cleveland to Columbus, Ohio.

Abraham Lincoln died on April 15, 1865. Six days later his body began a thirteen-day, 1,654-mile journey from Washington, D.C., to Springfield, Illinois. Along the way, the black-draped train stopped for public viewings at multiple cities. At each stop the president's coffin was removed and carried through the streets. It would be opened and hundreds of thousands of people would file past to say good-bye to their fallen leader.

In order to last the long trip, Lincoln's unrefrigerated body was embalmed. This new way

The funeral procession in New York City on April 25, 1865.

of preserving a dead body by replacing blood with chemicals was made popular during the Civil War. Lincoln's body had to be re-embalmed several times during the long journey.

The president was finally placed in his tomb at the Oak Ridge Cemetery in Springfield on May 4.

Every year on the anniversary of that bleak journey, **a ghost of the train** has been spotted on the rails between Washington and Illinois. At midnight the engine is said to appear out of the darkness, to the faint sound of funeral music.

THE PLOT TO STEAL LINCOLN'S BODY

In 1876 Chicago criminals planned to steal Lincoln's body from Springfield's Oak Ridge Cemetery. Their idea was to hold it for ransom in exchange for the release of a member of their gang from prison, as well as for $200,000. They might have succeeded if they hadn't hired a grave robber who was actually a paid informant of the Secret Service. They were captured after entering the tomb.

To stop any future grave robbers, a handful of Springfield residents secretly reburied Lincoln's coffin. It stayed in an unmarked grave in the tomb's basement until 1901, when Lincoln's son Robert asked that it be reburied securely. This time the body was housed inside a steel cage, placed inside a ten-foot-deep vault, and covered with thousands of pounds of concrete.

The burial service for President Lincoln at Oak Ridge Cemetery, Springfield, Illinois, on May 4, 1865.

MORE THAN 1,500 POWs
Perish on the Sultana

The overloaded steamboat Sultana *on the Mississippi River the day before her boilers exploded and she sank.*

What could be worse than enduring a bloody Civil War battle and a disease-ridden Confederate prison camp? What if you survived all of that only to die on your ride home? On April 27, 1865, as many as 1,700 passengers on the steamboat *Sultana* were killed when the ship's boilers exploded.

One boiler on the *Sultana* sprung a leak before the ship reached Vicksburg, Mississippi.

The boiler was quickly and poorly repaired so the vessel could take on the former prisoners. The government was paying five dollars a head to get them home and the captain wanted to make some quick money. **The vessel was only supposed to carry about four hundred men, but more than 2,100 were jammed aboard the 260-foot-long ship.**

The Sultana *goes up in flames as hundreds try to escape.*

On April 24 the overloaded ship left Vicksburg and began struggling up the swollen Mississippi River. Survivor Chester D. Berry remembered, "A happier lot of men I think I never saw than those poor fellows were. The most of them had been a long time in prison, some even for about two years, and the prospect of soon reaching home made them content to endure any amount of crowding."

Three days later outside of Memphis, Tennessee, the repaired boiler exploded at two a.m. Two more huge boilers soon followed. Survivor William Boor wrote, **"We were awakened by the exploding of the boilers of the boat, the cracking of timbers, wailing of men, and the screams and moaning from the wounded,** and the frantic men rushing to and fro, not knowing what to do, while the flames were madly rushing through the broken kindling of the boat cabin."

Those who escaped the **flames** by jumping into the river risked **drowning** in the strong current or **freezing to death** in the icy water.

They had no other choice, as there were only two small lifeboats and seventy-six life preservers on board. Men hit the chilly water in the dark and struggled to find a way out of the river, which was nearly four miles wide from flooding.

Of the approximately seven hundred who made it to shore, many were taken to hospitals. Sergeant William Fies of the Sixty-Fourth Ohio Infantry wrote that in his ward "the agonizing cries and groans of the burned and scalded were heartrending and almost unendurable, but in most cases the suffering was of short duration as most of them were relieved by death in a few hours." The fate of the *Sultana* is considered the worst maritime disaster in American history.

GREEDY INCOMPETENCE

Quartermaster Reuben Hatch, who was in charge of supplying food and materials to the military, was lucky to be the younger brother of Illinois politician Ozias M. Hatch, an advisor and close friend of President Lincoln. While he had previously been accused of taking bribes and later accused of fraud, Hatch somehow found himself the chief quartermaster, or officer, of the Department of Mississippi. He was the one who directed that the unreasonable amount of soldiers be put on the *Sultana*, even though other ships were available. Some claim he had received a huge payment from the ship's captain to send soldiers to the *Sultana*. Instead of being court-martialed and punished, Hatch was dismissed. No one ever went to jail for the disaster.

Hatch may have taken bribes in the form of cash, like this $5 bill from 1886.

The Stomach-Churning Filth
OF THE MEATPACKING INDUSTRY

The sausage-making machine at Swift & Co.'s Packing House in Chicago can stuff 10 feet per second. But what's really going into the sausage?

In 1865 leading meatpackers and railroads combined to create the Union Stock Yard and Transit Company. They built a centralized processing area south of Chicago, which was accessible by railroad. The huge stockyard, which covered nearly a square mile at its largest, received three million cattle and hogs in 1870 and twelve million in 1890. By 1900 Chicago meatpacking plants were among the largest factories in the United States and employed twenty-five thousand people.

The size and speed of packinghouses and their meat processing led to **dangerous levels of filth**, as well as **horrendous** working conditions.

Italian journalist Giuseppe Giacosa described workers on the cutting line covered in a mixture of animal grease and blood, which stained their faces and hardened in their hair, beards, and overalls so thick that it forced them to walk "with long stiff strides," like zombies.

In 1906 Upton Sinclair wrote a fictional story, *The Jungle*, to expose the horrible conditions of workers in the packinghouses. However, what really caught the public's attention was the poor health standards of the industry. **Sinclair wrote of animal carcasses riddled with worms or contaminated by disease and butchered in stomach-turning filth.**

One of the most quoted passages comes from chapter fourteen: "There was no place for the men to wash their hands before they ate their dinner, and so they made a practice of washing them in the water that was to be ladled into the sausage. There were the butt-ends of smoked

Workers dressing beef on the slaughtering floor.

meat, and the scraps of corned beef, and all the odds and ends of the waste of the plants, that would be dumped into old barrels in the cellar and left there . . . there were some jobs that it only paid to do once in a long time, and among these was the cleaning out of the waste barrels. Every spring they did it; and in the barrels would be dirt and rust and old nails and stale water—and cartload after cartload of it would be taken up and dumped into the hoppers with fresh meat, and sent out to the public's breakfast."

The public uproar over *The Jungle*

Swift and Co.'s station for splitting the ribs of pig carcasses.

washed, pushed from room to room in rotten box carts, in all of which processed it in the way of gathering dirt, splinters, floor filth, and the expectoration of tuberculous [*sic*] and other diseased workers." The justification for this treatment was that the meat would be sterilized when it was cooked, but much of it was not when it found its way into uncooked sausages.

The report led to the speedy passage of the Meat Inspection Act and Pure Food and Drug Act of 1906, through which the government required cleaner working conditions and proper labeling of meat.

caused President Theodore Roosevelt to launch an investigation. On June 2, 1906, he received a report from inspectors of the Chicago Stock Yards that he called "revolting." It read in part, "We saw meat shoveled from filthy wooden floors, piled on tables rarely

MEDICINE SO TERRIBLE IT COULD KILL YOU

While the meatpacking business was disgusting, the drug business at the time was deadly. In 1905 Samuel Hopkins Adams wrote a series for *Collier's Magazine* entitled "The Great American Fraud." In the articles he exposed how many of the medicines on the market didn't do what they claimed and included ingredients that could actually kill the user. He wrote that the American public's medicine contained "huge quantities of alcohol, an appalling amount of opiates and narcotics [drugs], a wide assortment of varied drugs ranging from powerful and dangerous heart depressants to insidious liver stimulants." One group of medicines he investigated was headache powders, many of which contained acetanilide, a drug that had the unfortunate side effect of causing heart failure! Adams's work also led to the passing of the Pure Food and Drug Act of 1906.

The Dismal Leper Colony
IN PARADISE

Residents of the Molokai leper settlement were banished there for life.

On January 6, 1866, a dozen people who were suffering from leprosy were left on the deserted island of Molokai, Hawaii. Ringed by lava rock and edged by cliffs, writer Robert Louis Stevenson called it a **"prison fortified by nature."** Its only contact with the outside world was ships that brought meager supplies and more people infected by leprosy.

At the time there was no medical treatment to stop the disease, which is caused by a bacterium. **Leprosy would start with a rash, which would then slowly spread over the body.** Victims would lose feeling in their hands, feet, and face. Many would go blind. Eventually it could kill you.

The only thing that could be done was quarantine the sick, which means keeping them away from healthy people.

Since the 1860s, about eight thousand leprosy sufferers have been taken from their families to live on Molokai. In the early years almost half of those left on the island died.

Missionary priests who came to ease the suffering of the island's residents sometimes contracted the disease themselves.

Writer Charles Warren Stoddard visited the island in 1884. When he first met the islanders, he "noticed that they were all disfigured: that **their faces were seared and scarred; their hands and feet maimed and sometimes bleeding;** their eyes like the eyes of some half-tamed animal; their mouths shapeless, and their whole aspect in many cases repulsive."

However, over the years doctors in the colony became more skilled. In 1908 writer Jack London visited the colony and wrote in *Women's Home Companion*, "One thing is certain. The leper in the settlement is far better off than the leper who lies in hiding outside. **Such a leper is a lonely outcast, living in constant fear of discovery and slowly and surely rotting away.**

The action of leprosy is not steady. It lays hold of its victim, commits a ravage, and then lies dormant for an indeterminate period. It may not commit another ravage for five years, or ten years, or forty years, and the patient may enjoy uninterrupted good health. Rarely, however, do these first ravages cease of themselves. The skilled surgeon is required, and the skilled surgeon cannot be called in for the leper who is in hiding."

While treatment for leprosy, now known as Hansen's disease, was available in the 1940s, many inflicted died from the disease. About seven thousand victims are buried on the tiny island.

POLIO TERRIFIES NEW YORK CITY

In 1916 the first large epidemic of polio hit New York City. Children were the most frequently affected, and the disease struck without warning. It would start like a cold, with a headache and chills. Then paralysis might set in, from just joints to your whole body. Some were suddenly unable to breathe or swallow, which quickly led to death. Because city authorities weren't sure how to stop it, they decided to forcibly separate sick children from their parents and place them in quarantine.

Streets were scrubbed, using four million gallons of water a day. Tens of thousands of stray animals were killed. But nothing could stop it. More than 9,000 cases were reported, which killed more than 2,300 people and paralyzed even more. The disease would mysteriously return every summer until a vaccine was created in 1955.

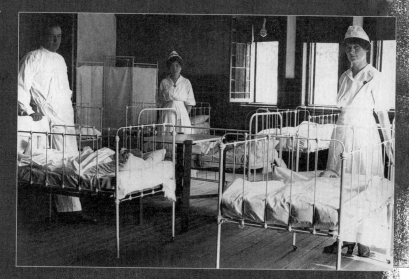

Infants afflicted with polio in a hospital ward in New York in 1916.

The Million Unvisited Graves ON HART ISLAND

In place of this cross, in 1948 burial duty inmates built a 30-foot-high memorial for the unclaimed dead, which has a cross on one side and the word "peace" on the other.

New York City has nearly 8.5 million residents, making it the most populous city in the United States. On Hart Island off the coast of the Bronx is the city's potter's field, which is also the most populous of its kind in the country.

This 101-acre cemetery is filled with 850,000 to one million people who died without family or enough money to be buried elsewhere.

After serving as a Civil War prison camp, the city bought the island in 1868 and established a potter's field, or a burial site for unknown or poor people. The first person buried there was Louisa Van Slyke, a twenty-four-year-old orphan who died alone in Charity Hospital. Since then between 1,500 and 2,000 are buried there each year. Before the bodies are taken by ferry to the island, a photo and fingerprints of each person are taken at the morgue. This is done because one-tenth of all bodies buried on Hart Island are people who are unidentified.

Currently, prison inmates from Riker's Island are paid to carry out the burials. For adult bodies, 150 coffins are stacked three-deep into seventy-foot-long pits, known as common graves. When there are children, which make up more than one-third of all burials, up to one thousand small coffins may fit in one grave. **They also bury amputated body parts, which are placed in boxes labeled "limbs."**

Because the prison department runs the island, for many years no one was allowed to visit. This changed in 2015, and now family members of the dead are allowed to visit one weekend a month.

Prisoners in 1890 loading coffins into an open trench on Hart Island.

THE SCARIEST CEMETERY IN AMERICA?

Wherever horror writer Edgar Allan Poe was buried after his untimely death at forty years old was bound to be creepy. But the Western Burial Ground at the Westminster Presbyterian Churchyard in Baltimore, Maryland, is not just creepy—it's terrifying. The ghosts of those accidentally buried alive during the cholera outbreaks (see page 106) are said to roam through the gravestones, looking for revenge. The spirit of a girl who died at age sixteen has repeatedly been seen kneeling in prayer at her own grave. The scariest story involves a minister who was murdered. When he was buried, it was said his skull never stopped screaming, even though it was later encased in a block of cement. The terrible sound is said to drive anyone who hears it insane.

PART IV: THE GILDED AGE AND THE PROGRESSIVE ERA (1870–1913)

1886 Statue of Liberty opens

Washington becomes a state **1889**

1898 U.S. declares war on Spain; Treaty of Paris is signed, ending the war and giving Puerto Rico and Guam to the U.S.; U.S. purchases the Philippines and annexes Hawaii (adds to U.S. Territory)

President McKinley assassinated; Vice President Theodore Roosevelt becomes president **1901**

1903 U.S. acquires the Panama Canal Zone and begins building; Wright brothers make their first flight

William Howard Taft begins term as president **1909**

1913 Woodrow Wilson begins term as president

the Raging fire that INCINERATED CHICAGO

One reason the blaze spread so quickly was because the water mains were dry after catching on fire. Firefighters were helpless to stop the fire until it began to rain.

To build a good fire, you need really dry wood. After the summer drought of 1871 lasted through the fall, Chicago's mostly wooden sidewalks and buildings, topped with flammable tar roofs, were the perfect fuel. **The city was only an oil lamp accident away from an inferno.**

And on the night of October 8, that's exactly what happened.

Around nine p.m. a small fire broke out in a barn on DeKoven Street. A mistake by the fire dispatcher sent firefighters in the wrong direction, giving the flames time to spread. Winds and intense heat helped the fire jump the river, sending it straight into the heart of the city.

"The firemen labored like heroes," the *Chicago Evening Post* reported on October 17. "Grimy, dusty, hoarse, soaked with water, time after time they charged up to the blazing foe only to be driven back to another position by its increasing fierceness, or to abandon as hopeless their task . . . **The people were mad . . . Seized with wild and causeless panics, they surged together, backwards and forwards, in the narrow streets, cursing, threatening, imploring, fighting to get free** . . . Everywhere, dust, smoke, flame, heat, thunder of falling walls, crackle of fire, hissing of water,

Julian Rumsey survived the fire, but his watch did not.

panting of engines, shouts, braying of trumpets, roar of wind, tumult, and uproar . . . **The storm howled with the fury of a maniac, the flames raged and roared with the unchained malice of a million fiends."**

Nearly three square miles of the inner city was destroyed, an estimated

The Chicago Chamber of Commerce and Crosby's Opera House in flames.

three hundred people were killed, and one-third of the population was left homeless. The reports of the fire moved as quickly as the flames. "By the morning of the 10th, within thirty-two hours of the first kindling of the flames in Chicago, fifty car-loads of provisions had arrived, to the relief of the destitute, some of them coming from towns three hundred miles away; and hundreds of thousands of dollars had been contributed," wrote Elias Colbert and Everett Chamberlin in their 1871 fire history, *Chicago and the Great Conflagration.* As soon as the ashes cooled, the city began to rebuild. An additional, smaller fire in 1874, which destroyed eight hundred buildings, ensured that future construction would be made with fireproof materials, such as stone and brick.

Some buildings in Chicago claimed to be fireproof, which led people to believe, incorrectly, that they would be safe on their roofs.

AN EVEN BIGGER FIRE

While the Chicago fire is the most well known of 1871, it wasn't even the largest fire on that *day.* In Wisconsin and Michigan, a dry spell combined with piles of wood and sawdust from logging and lumberyards led to the most deadly fire in American history. Strong winds sent the inferno roaring though the forest, killing between 1,200 and 2,500 people. More than one thousand died in the town of Peshtigo alone. One survivor, Reverend Peter Pernin, described the scene: "A thousand discordant deafening noises rose on the air together. The neighing of horses, falling of chimneys, crashing of up-rooted trees, roaring and whistling of the wind, crackling of fire as it ran with lightning-like rapidity from house to house—all sounds were there save that of human voice. People seemed stricken dumb by terror."

the plague of A BILLION LOCUSTS

A family capturing young grasshoppers during the plague, which could decimate fields of crops in a matter of hours.

A dark cloud traveled across the windless sky, blocking out the sun. While it sounded like rain, not a drop was felt in the dry fields. As farmers looked up from their plows, the locusts began to descend from the sky.

In 1874 billions of Rocky Mountain locusts, a type of grasshopper, formed the largest swarm in recorded history. The locusts cut a path estimated to be two million square miles from the eastern slope of the Rockies through to Texas. A *New York Times* reporter in Kansas wrote,

"The air is literally alive with them. They beat against the houses, swarm in at the windows, cover the passing trains. They work as if sent to destroy."

100

Author Laura Ingalls Wilder lived through a locust swarm and later wrote about it in *On the Banks of Plum Creek*: "A cloud was over the sun. It was not like any cloud they had ever seen before. It was a cloud of something like snowflakes, but they were larger than snowflakes, and thin and glittering. . . . The cloud was hailing grasshoppers. The cloud was grasshoppers. Their bodies hid the sun and made darkness. The rasping whirring of their wings filled the whole air and they hit the ground and the house with the noise of a hailstorm."

Laura Ingalls Wilder

a letter, Kansas settler E. Snyder wrote, "[The locusts] came—everywhere and on everything. By about four o'clock in the afternoon, every tree and bush, buildings, fences, fields, roads, and everything, except animated beings, was completely covered with grasshoppers."

Less than thirty years after filling the skies, the locusts disappeared.

The last Rocky Mountain locust was found in 1902. The species is now considered extinct.

The swarm caused $200 million in crop damage,

though the locusts ate most anything in their path, from clothes to grass to the wool off sheep! In

In 1871, the greatest nesting area of passenger pigeons covered 850 square miles in Wisconsin and was estimated to contain 136 million adult birds.

BILLIONS TO ZERO

In the nineteenth century, one out of every four birds in America was a passenger pigeon. The country's most abundant bird, it was found mainly east of the Rocky Mountains. When migrating, the flocks could number in the billions. John Jay Audubon, a famous bird artist, described seeing a flock in 1813: "The air was literally filled with Pigeons; the light of noon-day was obscured as by an eclipse; the dung fell in spots, not unlike melting flakes of snow; and the continued buzz of wings had a tendency to lull my senses to repose . . . Before sunset I reached Louisville, distant from Hardensburgh fifty-five miles. The Pigeons were still passing in undiminished numbers, and continued to do so for three days in succession." However, like the locust, the passenger pigeon's billions rapidly dwindled. Through hunting and loss of habitat, it became extinct in the early twentieth century. The last known passenger pigeon, named Martha after first lady Martha Washington, died in 1914 and is preserved and on display in the National Museum of Natural History in Washington, D.C.

WHITE HOUSE DOCTORS

Kill a President

More than a dozen renowned doctors' probing turned a 3-inch bullet wound into an infected 20-inch gash.

In 1880 Charles J. Guiteau supported underdog presidential nominee James Garfield by giving a few small speeches on his behalf. When Garfield surprisingly won, the mentally unstable lawyer expected big things in return. First Guiteau sent President Garfield a letter requesting an ambassadorship to Austria. Then he requested a posting in Paris. Neither request received a response. That's when Guiteau decided Garfield, who had only been president for four short months, had to die.

Guiteau decided to use a pistol, later saying, "[I] could creep up behind him and shoot him in the head, or through the body opposite the heart . . . **Of course I would be executed, but what of that, when I should become immortal and be talked of by all generations to come?**" At a train depot on

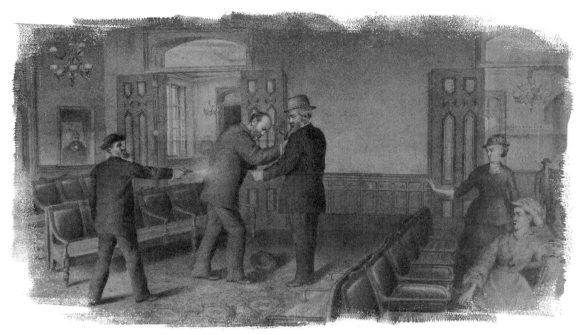

Two bullets from Guiteau's gun hit Garfield. One grazed his arm, while the other entered his back but did not exit.

July 2, 1881, he approached the unguarded president and shot him twice. "My God, what is this?" yelled Garfield as he fell to the ground.

Garfield might have lived, but doctors at the time didn't fully realize the danger of germs. As many as twelve doctors repeatedly stuck unwashed tools and hands into his wounds, causing massive infection. Every day he wasted away further in the summer heat (although what happened to him led to the invention of air-conditioning). The doctors stopped Garfield from eating food because they thought the bullet might have hit his intestines, weakening him further.

The president lost one hundred pounds in less than three months.

Alexander Graham Bell worked furiously to create a metal detector in hopes of finding the bullet still in him, which was lodged near Garfield's spine. When he had a working detector on July 26, he went to the president's bedside. "His face is very pale—or rather it is of an ashen gray color, which makes one feel for a moment that you are not looking upon a living man," Bell later wrote. However, Bell wasn't told that the president's bed had metal springs, which messed with the readings. Also, the doctor had him search in the wrong spot on Garfield for the bullet, so Bell's invention, which might have helped save the president, proved useless.

After eighty days of agony, Garfield finally died on September 19, 1881, at a seaside home in Long Branch, New Jersey. Guiteau was convicted of murder, though he stated, **"Yes, I shot him, but his doctors killed him."** While what he said was technically true, Guiteau was executed by hanging the following June.

CURSE OF TIPPECANOE

With few exceptions, every U.S. president since 1840 elected in years divisible by twenty has died in office. This trail of death supposedly originated when Shawnee Indian chief Tecumseh was killed fighting William Henry Harrison's troops. After the Battle of Tippecanoe, Tecumseh's half brother, known as the Prophet, was said to have cursed Harrison and every "white chief" chosen in twenty-year succession. History seems to prove this:

1840 William Henry Harrison: died of pneumonia

1860 Abraham Lincoln: assassinated

1880 James A. Garfield: assassinated

1900 William McKinley: assassinated

1920 Warren G. Harding: died from either a heart attack or stroke

1940 Franklin D. Roosevelt: died of a cerebral brain hemorrhage

1960 John F. Kennedy: assassinated

When Ronald Reagan was elected in 1980, the prophecy was on everyone's mind. However, President Reagan survived an assassination attempt in 1981, which appears to have broken the curse.

The death of Tecumseh at the Battle of Thames in 1813.

CHOLERA AND THE FEAR of Being Buried Alive

"A Premature Burial" by artist Antoine Wiertz shows a cholera victim awakening in a coffin.

Turn-of-the-century doctors lacked the medical technology to determine if people were truly dead, not just in a deep coma. Also, cholera outbreaks at the time meant people were buried quickly to prevent the spread of the disease. Because mistakes were sometimes made, **being buried alive in the late 1800s was a legitimate concern.**

Popular fiction, such as Edgar Allan Poe's "The Premature Burial" and Wilkie Collins's *Jezebel's Daughter*, helped fan the fear. A story in the *New York Times* on February 9, 1884, detailed one such case, which began with the abrupt and unexpected death of Anna Hochwalt of Dayton, Ohio, on the day her brother Edward was getting married.

The story read, "The examination showed that Anna was of excitable temperament, nervous, and affected with sympathetic palpitation of the heart. Dr. Jewett thought this was the cause of her supposed death. On the following day, the lady was interred in the Woodland. The friends of Miss Hochwalt were unable to forget the terrible impression and **several ladies observed that her eyes bore a remarkably** natural **color and could not dispel an idea that she was not dead.** They conveyed their opinion to Anna's parents and the thought preyed upon them so that the body was taken from the grave. It was stated that when the coffin was opened it was discovered that the supposed inanimate body had turned upon its right side.

The hair had been torn out in handfuls and the flesh had been bitten from the fingers."

Anna was only nineteen years old when she was buried alive. Once proven dead, the body was reburied and the family tried to keep the story quiet. However, word got out in the media, and Anna's story only increased the public's fears.

The gravestone of Anna Hochwalt, who died for good in 1884.

SAFETY COFFINS

In response to people's fears of being buried alive, inventors created safety coffins. These had devices built in so the dead could signal the outside world if they awoke underground. In 1897 Count de Karnice-Karnicki of Russia created a device that provided oxygen to the coffin and used a flag and bell system triggered by movement to alert those aboveground. He traveled the world touting his invention, but a demonstration in which he buried an assistant alive went terribly wrong. The assistant's brush with death ruined the count's chances of selling any of his inventions.

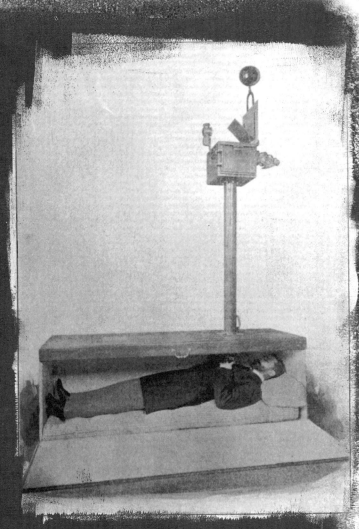

The goal of the safety coffin was to "do away with the uncertainty of establishing death and save people buried alive."

THE GREAT
White Hurricane

The awning of a grocery store collapsed under the weight of the snow during the blizzard of 1888 in New York City.

On March 11, 1888, a storm came out of nowhere and paralyzed the northeast United States. Winds gusted as high as seventy miles per hour. In some places fifty-two inches of snow dropped in thirty-six hours. **Drifts fifty feet high covered the doors of homes.**

A *Harper's Weekly* reporter in New York City wrote, "The snow was fine and dry and copious, and was driven by a gale from the west and north. The city had known higher winds and snowfalls as heavy, but never a combination which was so furious. At four o'clock in the morning the snow came so fast that five minutes sufficed to obliterate the footprints of a man or a horse in the streets.

A scene showing the terrible force of the wind in Printing House Square in New York City.

and electrical wires were ripped apart by wind and ice. Trains filled with passengers were stuck on tracks. Scores of boats were sunk by the high winds and waves. The East River was almost totally blocked by ice. **Hundreds of foolish people used the shifting ice as a bridge to get to and from Brooklyn, as it was the only way across.**

A reporter for the *New York Times* wrote in amazement that "the elements were able to overcome the boasted triumph of civilization . . . It is hard to believe in this last quarter of the nineteenth century that for even one day New York could be so completely isolated from the rest of the world as

At sunrise the city was snowed under. . . . Those who could open their front door in the morning, without admitting a snowdrift of a very respectable size, poked their heads out for a moment, and in a majority of cases decided to stay home for that day, and let business run itself."

From Maine to Maryland more than four hundred people were killed. In New York City the Stock Exchange closed for two days— one of the few times in history. Overhead telegraph, telephone,

Carts haul snow and ice from the streets to be dumped in the East River.

if Manhattan Island was in the middle of the South Sea." In the city, the mountains of snow were shoveled by hand into carts and then dumped in the river. It took days for the trains to run again, which was one reason New York City would eventually build an underground subway system.

TOP FIVE DEADLIEST WINTER STORMS

1. 1888 - Northeast states - Death toll: 400+
2. 1950 - Eastern states - Death toll: 353
3. 1993 - Eastern states - Death toll: 270
4. 1913 - Great Lakes - Death toll: 250
5. 1888 - Midwestern states - Death toll: 235

The Appalling World of BABY FARMS

FIND 21 INFANTS DIED IN YEAR AT BABY FARM; DIG YARD FOR GRAVES

BUTLER TO URGE FORTIFICATION OF HAWAIIAN ISLES

Will Make Them "Strongest" Military Outpost in World—To Study Plan.

Washington, May 8 (AP).—Chairman Butler of the House Naval Committee said today he would urge legislation at the next session of Congress to make the Hawaiian Islands...

"Baby Farm" Proprietor Faces Homicide Charge

One More Victim of Mrs. Geisen-Volk's Infantorium in E. 86th St., Manhattan, Died Today — Startling Disclosures Expected as Arraignment of Woman, Held in $35,000 Bail, Is Postponed.

The discovery that no less than 21 infants have died in little more than a year at the "baby farm" conducted by Mrs. Helen Auguste Geisen-Volk...

Before there was a system in place, desperate, often unwed mothers or widowed fathers would sometimes place their children in "baby farms" to be taken care of for a fee. The arrangement was either temporary, like today's day care, or permanent, like an orphanage. However, some who ran baby farms realized they could make more money if they let the children die, either through neglect or by more terrible means.

Reverend Benjamin Waugh, who founded the National Society for the Prevention of Cruelty to Children in the United Kingdom, wrote in 1890 of the worst of the baby farms he had investigated: "Crouching and sprawling on the floor, in their own excrement, were two of them. **The stench of the room was so abominable that a grown man vomited on opening the door of it.** Though three were nearly two years old, none of them could walk. In bitter March, there was no fire . . . All were yellow, fevered, skin and bone. None of them cried, they were too weak . . . A man and his wife sat watching them die of filth and famine, so making their living."

Helen Auguste Geisen-Volk ran a baby farm on East 86th Street in New York City. When William Angerer came to visit his son, who was in her care, she couldn't

PROGRESS

produce the seven-month-old baby and then tried to substitute another child for his son. Once police began their investigation, they found that a number of babies in Geisen-Volk's care had died from malnutrition and neglect. A nurse who worked at the baby farm testified that Geisen-Volk had slammed a baby against the wall because it wouldn't stop crying. She was also said to beat babies whose parents were behind in their payments. In total she was charged with the murder of fifty-three babies. **The judge called her "cruel and bestial" and a "revolting anomaly in humankind"** before sentencing her to a mere three to seven years in Auburn Prison.

ORPHAN TRAINS

With disease and poverty killing many adults, New York City in the 1850s had thousands of abandoned and homeless children roaming the streets. There was no system in place to help them.

An orphan train makes a stop around 1900.

Claretta Miller, who was nine years old at the time, remembered her life in the city: "We were hungry. We slept on old, dirty mattresses on the floor and the rats ran over our heads and through our hair lots of nights and we'd wake up screaming with it. We don't know where our parents were. We never did know." In response a minister named Charles Loring Brace founded the Children's Aid Society, with the goal of getting children off the streets and into safe homes. He organized children to take train trips to small towns throughout America, where they were taken in by families. Many also went to work on farms, which were desperate for workers. Some children ended up with nice families, while others were beaten and ran away. Between 1854 and 1929 more than one hundred thousand children were sent out of New York on these orphan trains.

TUBERCULOSIS AND THE Last American Vampire

Doctors would try anything to cure tuberculosis, including giving a direct blood transfusion from a goat in 1891.

Tuberculosis, known as the "white death," was a terrifying plague. In the early 1900s, **it killed one out of every seven people in the United States.** People stricken with the disease became weak with fever and coughed until they basically drowned in their own blood.

In the 1880s a Rhode Island farmer named George Brown stood by helplessly as tuberculosis killed both his wife and his daughter Mary. At the time no one knew what caused it or how to stop it. Around 1891 Brown's son, Edwin, got sick. The next year one of George's other teenage daughters, Mercy, died from tuberculosis as well. How could he defend what remained of his family?

After Mercy's funeral in January, Edwin became sicker. George grasped for ways to save his son. In desperation he began to listen to rumors that those with tuberculosis were actually victims of a vampire attack. Both made a person become pale, stop eating, and seem like the life was being drained out of them. Maybe his daughter Mercy wasn't dead but was a vampire preying on Edwin.

When George opened Mercy's coffin at Chestnut Hill Cemetery, she looked surprisingly alive. This seemed strange because she'd been dead for months and hadn't been embalmed. What looked like fresh blood was found in her heart. George started to believe Mercy really was a vampire. (Or maybe her body had just been stored aboveground in freezing weather.)

To end Mercy's power over Edwin, George did what folklore

NOT THE ONLY VAMPIRE

The scourge of tuberculosis caused more than one family to mistake the dead for a vampire. In 1817 Frederick Ransom, a Dartmouth College student, died. When the rest of his family started to get sick, his father had him dug up and his heart burned in a blacksmith's fire. It didn't work, because his mother, sister, and two of his brothers died soon afterward.

claimed killed vampires—**he cut out her heart, burned it, and fed the ashes to his son.** Edwin still died within two months, on May 2, 1892.

Edwin was one of many killed by tuberculosis. In 1884 sanitariums began to be founded in healthy locations to help combat the disease. By 1910 one in seventy Americans lived in a sanitarium and in some places, like Colorado, sixty percent of the population had tuberculosis or was related to someone who did. The disease killed an estimated 110,000 a year in the U.S., before effective medicines were developed in 1943.

Mercy Brown was only nineteen years old when she died.

The Pinkertons' Deadly Bungling
OF THE HOMESTEAD STRIKE

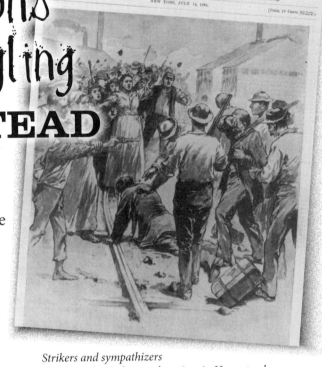

Strikers and sympathizers attacking the Pinkerton detectives in Homestead.

The Pinkerton National Detective Agency was formed by Allan Pinkerton in 1850. They began by investigating train robberies but became famous when they foiled an assassination plot against Abraham Lincoln in 1861. Allan went on to work with Union general George McClellan during the Civil War, compiling information on the Confederates.

By 1890 the Pinkerton Agency was huge, with two thousand active agents and thirty thousand reserves, making it bigger than the United States' standing army at the time. Because of growing problems with workers, companies began hiring Pinkerton detectives to spy on labor unions and help business owners stop labor strikes. This led to one of the most unfortunate incidents in the agency's history.

On July 6, 1892, three hundred Pinkerton detectives were sent to Carnegie Steel in Homestead, Pennsylvania. Plant manager Henry

The motto of the Pinkerton Agency is "We Never Sleep" and their logo features an unblinking eye. This is the origin of the term "private eye."

C. Frick was at a standoff with the striking Amalgamated Association of Iron and Steel Workers union and had called in the Pinks, as they were known, to provide muscle. When they tried to sneak in by tugboat in the cover of night, they were greeted by thousands of furious strikers. Both sides were armed and shots were immediately fired.

The sheriff of Homestead refused to send his deputies, telling *The Evening World*, **"I believe it would be suicidal for me to take my men there. We could not hope to cope with five thousand men."** The gunfight continued until the governor sent in the Pennsylvania militia.

In the end nine workers and three Pinkerton detectives were dead. The union was effectively broken. While Andrew Carnegie, the wealthy owner of the steel company, had initially condoned, or approved, Frick's actions, he later regretted it, writing, "This is the trial of my life (death's hand excepted).

Such a foolish step—contrary to my ideals, repugnant [disgusting] to every feeling of my nature."

OVERZEALOUS PURSUIT OF OUTLAWS

In the 1870s the Pinkerton detectives were known for their pursuit of notorious outlaws, especially bank and train robber Jesse James. In January 1875 they planned a raid on the James family farm in Missouri. The flares they threw into the house exploded, accidentally killing James's eight-year-old half brother, Archie, and blowing their mother's arm off. The story appeared in newspapers across the country, causing the agency to stop its hunt for Jesse James. He was later killed by one of his own gang for the reward money.

Jesse James's family farm, where the outlaw was originally buried upon his death in 1882. His mother used to sell rocks from his grave to tourists for a quarter.

The Living Exhibits AT THE WORLD'S FAIR

The center of the fair was known as the White City for its white stucco siding and streets lit by electric lights.

PROGRESS

From May 1 to the end of October in 1893, Chicago hosted the World's Columbian Exposition, which was visited by twenty-seven million people. Timed to coincide with the four hundredth anniversary of Christopher Columbus's voyage, it opened a year late after three frantic years of preparation. The 630 acres were packed with marvels and curiosities, including an eleven-ton block of cheese and an eighty-two-foot-high tower of light, with a top made from 30,000 pieces of cut glass. Many products were introduced there for the first time, such as Cracker Jacks and Juicy Fruit gum.

The Midway was home to the more popular attractions, including "primitive" cultures on display. One of the most visited was an entire Javanese village from Indonesia.

One hundred twenty-five people were brought to live in Chicago from West Java for five months in order to promote the area's coffee and tea. On the front porches women demonstrated dying fabric, weaving, and embroidery. In the center of the village was a mosque where the faithful were called to prayer by a large drum. Warm drinks were dispensed from a teahouse.

The Cairo section of the Midway, built to resemble the ancient city, was popular because people could ride camels and watch exotic dancers.

THE PYGMY AT THE ZOO

Ota Benga

In September 1906 a penniless four-foot-eleven-inch member of a Congolese pygmy tribe named Ota Benga arrived at the Bronx Zoo. He was dressed in modern clothes but shoeless, and his teeth were sharpened into points. He had come to America to appear in the 1904 World's Fair and had stayed.

When Benga's sponsor ran out of money, zoo director William Temple Hornaday offered to take him in, along with his pet chimpanzee. Benga helped with the monkeys and was encouraged to set up a hammock in the Monkey House. Once word got out, thousands flocked to see him. The *Evening Post* reported, he "has a great influence with the beasts—even with the larger kind, including the orangutan with whom he plays as though one of them, rolling around the floor of the cages in wild wrestling matches and chattering to them in his own guttural tongue, which they seem to understand." While his fame grew so did the outrage of exhibiting a man as if he were an animal. By the end of the month, he left the zoo and was taken in by the Howard Colored Orphan Asylum.

The one-thousand-seat bamboo theater had nearly 82,000 visitors during the Exposition. In the evenings an instrument called the gamelan accompanied performances of two types of wayang, which were plays combining puppetry and human dance that tell stories of heroism in Javanese culture. One report stated, "They were most interesting, these gentle Javanese, and, in certain ways and habits and view of life, quite unlike any other people in the world, so far as the Fair afforded an illustration."

At the fair's end, most of the village was bought by the Field Museum and the workers went back to their country.

The Javanese Gamelan Orchestra and Topeng masked dancers at the World's Columbian Exposition.

Hundreds Burn in the
HOBOKEN DOCKS FIRE

The SS Bremen drifted ablaze from the Hoboken docks.

In the late afternoon on June 30, 1900, Pier 3 in Hoboken, New Jersey, was flanked with four great ocean liners. Stacked on the docks were bales of cotton and barrels of turpentine and oil. A fire broke out, spreading rapidly along the wooden pier, fanned by the stiff breeze and increased by the oil barrels that burst in the heat.

"The scene half an hour after the starting of the fire beggared all description," the *New York Times* reported the next day. "The *Kaiser Wilhelm der Grosse*, the pride of the line, was towed slowly away, afire at several places and her crew valiantly fighting to save the vessel. The *Saale* and the *Bremen* followed, drifting helplessly, flames bursting out in every part of the ship, **men jumping overboard, and others, caught as in traps, trying in vain to force their way through the small portholes, while the flames pressed relentlessly upon them.**"

The *Kaiser Wilhelm der Grosse* was quickly emptied of passengers and crew. Tugboats pulled the burning ship away from the pier. The crews from the *Saale* and *Bremen* liners cut ties to the pier. Tug and fireboats streamed water as desperate crewmembers, many unable to swim, jumped from the decks into the sea.

The last liner, the *Main*, burned at the pier, with many of the crew trapped inside. "It lay there in a cauldron of flames, with its many victims, some of whom were seen trying to get out of the portholes, when the smoke drew a curtain over the ghastly scene," reported the *New York Times*. When a tugboat pulled next to the ship, sixteen men miraculously crawled out of the smoking ruins. They had locked themselves in an empty coal bunker and somehow survived.

At least 326 people were killed, with a total of more than $6 million in damages.

GHOST SHIP

While more than sixty-five people died on the liner *Saale*, it was later refitted and became a cargo ship under the name SS *J. L. Luckenbach*. According to authors Troy Taylor and Rene Kruse, crews called it unlucky, and others claimed it was haunted. Screams and footsteps were heard in empty corridors. During World War I in 1917, the ship was attacked by a German submarine. While the flames were being extinguished, shrieking was heard from an empty hold where many had perished in Hoboken. The ghostly figure of a woman in a long burning dress was also seen. Creepiest of all, the crew of the ship that came to the rescue of the *Luckenbach* saw women frantically signaling in the portholes of the ship. But there were no women on board—just the ghosts of the Hoboken fire.

GALVESTON, AMERICA'S
Deadliest Natural Disaster

The shattered remains of a high school in Galveston.

At the end of the nineteenth century, Galveston was the biggest city in Texas, with more than 36,000 residents, many of them millionaires. The bustling port city had escaped serious damage in numerous storms, making residents feel somewhat invincible. When the U.S. Weather Bureau's Isaac Cline was asked if any hurricane posed a threat to the city, he replied it was "an absurd delusion."

On September 8, 1900, that delusion came roaring out of the Gulf of Mexico in the form of an extreme hurricane. Winds reached 130 to 140 miles per hour and created a storm surge in excess of fifteen feet (seven feet higher than the tallest point in Galveston). Houses collapsed and the storm

John Blagden, who worked at the Weather Bureau in Galveston, wrote, "The more fortunate are doing all they can to aid the sufferers but it is impossible to care for all. . .We have neither light, fuel or water."

drove the debris over the island, crushing everything in its path. In Cline's memoir, he wrote, "The battle for our lives, against the elements and the terrific hurricane winds and storm-tossed wreckage, lasted from eight p.m. until near midnight **. . . with only an occasional flash of lightning which revealed the terrible carnage about us."**

When the hurricane finally passed, at least 8,000 people were dead, 3,600 buildings were destroyed, and damage estimates exceeded $20 million, which would be more than $700 million in today's dollars. Traveling salesman Charles Law wrote to his wife, "I have passed through the most trying, horrible thing in my life. God knows that on Saturday night at nine o'clock I had given up all hopes of ever seeing the light of day . . . **it seemed that I would be floating with the thousand poor dead bodies out in the streets at any moment** . . . On Sunday morning, after the storm was all over . . . I gazed upon dead bodies lying here and there. The houses all blown to pieces; women, men, and children all walking the streets in a weak condition with bleeding heads and bodies and feet all torn to pieces with glass."

Horse carts piled with bodies made their way through the shattered streets of Galveston. The corpses were placed on barges and buried together at sea. But, like a never-ending nightmare, the water's current kept bringing them back to shore. Finally townspeople began burning bodies in huge funeral pyres. Emma Bernie Beal would be haunted for years by the sight: "I stood out there and watched them burn some bodies . . . I recall this one body, the arm went up like that and I screamed. I never will forget that . . . I'd have nightmares and scream and holler . . . There's something crazy about you when you watch anything like that."

To this day the 1900 Galveston hurricane remains the deadliest natural disaster in American history.

A small passageway amid the debris on 19th Street in Galveston.

TOP FIVE DEADLIEST HURRICANES

1. 1900 – Galveston, TX - Death toll: 8,000 to 12,000

2. 1928 – Okeechobee, FL - Death toll: 2,500 to 3,000

3. 2005 – Louisiana and Mississippi ("Katrina") - Death toll: 1,800

4. 1893 – South Carolina and Georgia - Death toll: 1,000 to 2,000

5. 1893 – Louisiana – Death toll: 1,100 to 1,400

Six Hundred Die in Ten Minutes

IN "FIREPROOF" THEATER

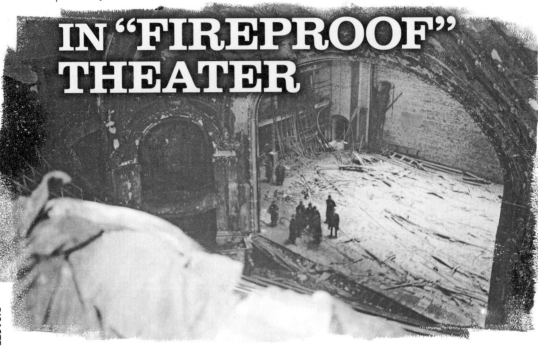

A view of the burned stage from the balcony, where hundreds became trapped and died.

"Is there any living person here?"

a fire marshal kept shouting. Twenty minutes before, the overflow crowd of nearly two thousand people had been enjoying the bargain matinee of *Mr. Bluebeard* at the Iroquois Theater in Chicago, Illinois. Now the hundreds who weren't lucky enough to escape America's worst theater fire were dead. Caused by an arc light igniting a curtain, the fire swept through the theater, fed by drafts caused when doors opened.

Eddie Foy, who appeared in the play that day, later wrote, "The flame spread through those tinderlike fabrics with terrible rapidity ... Within a minute, the flame was beyond

possibility of control by anything but a fire hose.

"The crowd was beginning to surge toward the doors and already showing signs of a stampede—those on the lower floor were not so badly frightened as those in the more dangerous balcony and gallery. Up there, they were falling into panic . . . **I could see them surging, fighting, milling about in the flickering light, a horde of maniacs.**"

An asbestos curtain designed to stop the fire from reaching the audience snagged on its way down. Many exits were hard to find, doors were bolted shut, and there were no sprinklers or fire alarms in the building. While burns and smoke inhalation accounted for many of the 602 dead, including 212 children, **others were trampled to death in the panic.**

Foy wrote, "The stairways were one long mass of bodies, and wherever turns or landings caused a worse jam, they were piled seven or eight feet deep. Firemen and police confronted a sickening task in disentangling them . . . The heel

A panorama view of the interior of the Iroquois Theater shows the damage from the deadly fire.

prints on the dead faces mutely testified to the cruel fact that **human animals stricken by terror are as mad and ruthless as stampeding cattle."**

Chicago Fire Department's Engine 13 arrived quickly but it was too late, as the theater had no sprinklers, alarms, or water connections.

The opulent Chicago theater went up in flames so fast that Foy claimed the entire fire lasted only eight minutes. Surprisingly, with the vast number of casualties and poor fire protection of the theater, no one was convicted of any crime. However, in the wake of the 1903 tragedy, fire codes throughout the country were changed to require theater doors to open outwards, and to have clearly marked exits and fire curtains made of steel.

TOP FIVE DEADLIEST BUILDING FIRES

1. 1903 - Iroquois Theater Chicago, IL - Death toll: 602
2. 1942 - Cocoanut Grove nightclub, Boston, MA - Death toll: 492
3. 1930 - Ohio State Penitentiary, Columbus, OH - Death toll: 320
4. 1876 - Brooklyn Theater, Brooklyn, NY - Death toll: 285
5. 1940 - Rhythm Club, Natchez, MS - Death toll: 207

WESTINGHOUSE AND EDISON'S

War of the Currents

George Westinghouse

Thomas Edison

Thomas Edison was a genius, although sometimes an evil one.

His evil side was evident in his competition with rival George Westinghouse. When he couldn't prove that his direct current (DC) electric system was better than George Westinghouse's alternating current (AC) system, Edison plotted the most effective way he could to sway the public—by killing animals.

George Westinghouse wrote, "I remember Tom [Edison] telling them that direct current was like a river flowing peacefully to the sea, while alternating current was like a torrent rushing violently over a precipice. Imagine that! Why they even had a professor named Harold Brown who went

129

around talking to audiences . . . and electrocuting dogs and old horses right on stage, to show how dangerous alternating current was."

Edison's most brutal display was the 1903 electrocution of an elephant, which had recently trampled three men. The *New York Times* wrote, "Topsy, the big, man-killing elephant at Luna Park, Coney Island, paid the death penalty at the park yesterday by the agency of a heavy electric current and 460 grains of cyanide of potassium." Edison's company even filmed the poor pachyderm's death so it could be seen by more than that day's small crowd.

While Edison opposed capital punishment, he had a hand in the creation of the electric chair. Harold Brown, who had electrocuted the animals, built the first electric chair. Edison secretly paid Brown to use AC current in the design. **Edison even attempted to get people to use "Westinghoused" as another word for being executed.**

The first person to be condemned to death by electrocution was William Kemmler, who had murdered his wife. When he was strapped into the chair on August 6, 1890, the first jolt of seventeen seconds of electricity was not enough to kill him. The second, four-minute jolt not only caused his death, but caused his head to smoke. Westinghouse later commented, "They would have done better using an axe."

Topsy the elephant was fed poison-laced carrots, then tied down and electrocuted.

The original electric chair was first used in New York, then later moved to Tennessee.

Westinghouse eventually won the war of public opinion by winning the bid to light the World's Columbian Exposition in Chicago in 1893 (see page 118), an ideal showcase for electricity. The fair, attended by more than twenty-seven million people, was opened when President Grover Cleveland pressed a button to turn on more than one hundred thousand lightbulbs.

THE UNHOLY LIGHTNING ROD

Benjamin Franklin began experimenting with electricity after hearing a lecture about it in 1743. His creation of the lightning rod—which directs the energy from lightning into the ground, decreasing the likelihood of a house fire—was the first practical application of electricity. Franklin considered it his greatest invention.

Churches were often struck by lightning, as their steeples were the highest points in towns, so you'd think they would be grateful for the invention. Yet some church elders felt Franklin's invention was attempting to "control the artillery of heaven." Franklin scoffed at the argument, asking if it was against God's will to build a roof to keep out the rain as well.

Benjamin Franklin's first lightning rod was in Philadelphia on the house of Benjamin West, a banker.

the fiery End
OF
THE GENERAL SLOCUM

The wreck of the General Slocum.

On June 15, 1904, people excitedly boarded the steamer *General Slocum* for a ride up New York City's East River to a picnic ground on Long Island's North Shore. The 1,358 passengers were mainly women and children, most from Kleindeutschland, or Little Germany, on Manhattan's Lower East Side.

A fire was noticed onboard near Ninety-Seventh Street but the crew was unable to put it out. Fearing the boat would set fire to the lumber stored on the pier at 134th Street, the captain pushed the steamer toward North Brother Island, a mile away. Wind, combined with the ship's speed, just fanned the flames.

Passenger Reverend Julius G. Schulz of Erie, Pennsylvania, told the *New York Times*, **"The flames spread so rapidly and it seemed only a second before the whole craft was ablaze from end to end.** Women and children jumped in the wildest manner to their deaths, while the efforts of the mothers to save their little ones was the most heartrending spectacle I have ever witnessed."

The crew had never had a fire drill. While there were enough life jackets, the cork inside them had turned to dust because of age. Fire hoses burst when used. Lifeboats were stuck to the deck by layers of paint because they had never been moved during deck painting. Most of the passengers did not know how to swim and wore layers of heavy clothes, which weighed them down when they hit the water. Those who could swim were often dragged under by those panicking in the water.

Bodies washed up on the shore of North Brother Island for days. In total 1,021 out of the 1,358 passengers died.

HAUNTED ISLAND

When the *General Slocum* beached off North Brother Island, the only inhabitants were patients quarantined in the Riverside Hospital for infectious diseases, as well as the doctors and nurses who cared for them. Their illnesses did not stop many from plunging into the river to help save those fleeing from the burning ship. While some were saved, many more perished.

Eventually the hospital closed and the building was abandoned. Some say the spirits of those who perished that day, as well as many who died of diseases, still haunt the hospital's empty hallways.

Dozens of bodies line the shore of North Brother Island.

San Francisco's trifecta of terror:
EARTHQUAKE, FIRE, AND PLAGUE

Armed policemen patrol the ruined streets, while fires still burn in the wake of the earthquake.

At 5:12 a.m. on April 18, 1906, a huge earthquake hit San Francisco that measured between 7.7 and 8.3 on the Richter scale. The largest earthquake ever recorded using this scale, which measures the impact of how powerful a quake is, was a 9.5.

John Barrett, news editor of the *San Francisco Examiner,* was leaving work on Market Street when it hit: "[All] of a sudden we had found ourselves staggering and reeling. It was as if the earth was slipping gently from under our feet. Then came the sickening swaying of the earth that threw us flat upon our faces . . . We could not get on our feet. Then it

seemed as though my head were split with the roar that crashed into my ears. **Big buildings were crumbling as one might crush a biscuit in one's hand...** Wild, high jangles of smashing glass cut a sharp note into the frightful roaring. Ahead of me a great cornice [piece of a building] crushed a man as if he were a maggot . . . It seemed a quarter of an hour until it stopped. As a matter of fact, it lasted only three minutes."

The next day the *New York Times* reported, "The people became panic-stricken, and rushed

Many buildings were shaken from their foundations. A businessman wrote that "a twelve-story skyscraper, stood and looked all right at first glance, but had moved at the base two feet at one end out into the sidewalk, and the elevators refused to work, all the interior being just twisted out of shape."

into the streets, most of them in their night attire. They were met by showers of falling bricks, cornices, and walls of buildings. Many were crushed to death, while others were badly mangled. Those who remained indoors generally escaped with their lives, though scores were hit by detached plaster, pictures, and articles thrown to the floor by the shock. It is believed that more or less loss was sustained by nearly every family in the city."

The fire approached the hospital near the Union Ferry Building.

More than three thousand people died, and approximately 250,000 were left homeless by the earthquake and ensuing fires that raged for four days. The tens of thousands who couldn't leave the city were housed in tents in public spaces. They stood in long lines for food and had to cook in communal stoves in the streets. Eventually, the army would house twenty thousand refugees in some of the city's twenty-six military-style tent camps. Some were still there two years later.

TOP FIVE DEADLIEST AMERICAN EARTHQUAKES

1. 1906 - San Francisco, CA - Death toll: 3,000+
2. 1964 - Prince William Sound, Alaska - Death toll: 131
3. 1933 - Long Beach, CA - Death toll: 115
4. 1989 - San Francisco Bay Area, CA - Death toll: 67
5. 1886 - Charleston, SC - Death toll: 60

TYPHOID MARY, Serving Up Death One family at a time.

This illustration in a 1909 newspaper explained how typhoid could easily be spread by Mary as she cooked.

Irish-born cook Mary Mallon was known for her peach ice cream. Her cold specialty is also thought to be the way she spread typhoid fever, a form of salmonella that can cause fever, diarrhea, and death.

While Mallon herself was immune to the disease, the dozens of families she cooked for were not. And, as was the practice of the day, she rarely washed her hands. If she served food that was not hot enough to kill the germs, those eating it would become infected. During her twelve-year career, she is thought to have infected fifty-one people and killed at least three of them.

Sanitary engineer George Soper was hired by one of the families to find out where they had contracted typhoid. When he tracked Mallon down in 1907 in the kitchen of a New York City family where she now cooked, she chased him out with a

The tiny bungalow on North Brother Island where Mary lived alone for the rest of her life.

carving knife. Five policemen came back to wrestle her into custody.

Mary was quarantined for three years in a bungalow of Riverside Hospital on North Brother Island. There they verified that she had the disease. In order to be released, she promised never to cook for others again. However, she didn't have any symptoms and few other skills. So a few years later she was cooking again.

In 1915 Mary was apprehended after she caused an outbreak at a maternity hospital, where she cooked under a fake name. She was sent back to the island for twenty-three more years until she died of a stroke.

THE TERROR OF TYPHOID FEVER

During the Civil War, two percent of the entire Union army died of typhoid fever, totaling more than twenty-seven thousand men. Soldiers who contracted the disease had high fevers, weakness, intense headaches, red rashes, stomach issues, and delirium. Often transmitted by body lice, it was the second highest killer during the war. Doctors at that time had no way to combat the bacteria that caused the disease.

Private Samuel Wires, who contracted typhoid fever while serving in the Indiana Infantry Regiment, was sent home weighing only 90 pounds, and died three weeks later at the age of seventeen.

the Shocking truth
OF CHILD LABOR

Group of Breaker boys. Smallest is Sam Belloma, Pine Street. Pittston, Pennsylvania.

Lewis Hine, a former schoolteacher, became the photographer for the National Child Labor Committee. This group hoped to reform the use of children in factories, mines, fields, and other occupations. His series of photographs between 1908 and 1912 were created to show the public the harsh working conditions and help change the nation's labor laws.

He wrote, **"There is work that profits children, and there is work that brings profit only to employers.** The object of employing children is not to train them, but to get high profits from their work." The captions to the above and following images are Hine's.

FURMAN OWENS, *twelve years old. Can't read. Doesn't know his ABCs. Said, "Yes, I want to learn but can't when I work all the time." Been in the mills four years, three years in the Olympia Mill.*
Columbia, South Carolina.

One of the spinners in Whitnel Cotton Mill. She was fifty-one inches high. Has been in the mill one year. Sometimes works at night. Runs four sides—forty-eight cents a day. When asked how old she was, she hesitated, then said, "I don't remember," then added confidentially, "I'm not old enough to work, but do just the same." Out of fifty employees, there were ten children about her size.
Whitnel, North Carolina.

TONY CASALE, *age eleven, been selling four years. Sells sometimes until ten p.m. His paper told me the boy had shown him the marks on his arm where his father had bitten him for not selling more papers. He (the boy) said, "Drunken men say bad words to us."*
Hartford, Connecticut.

View of the Ewen Breaker of the Pennsylvania Coal Co. The dust was so dense at times as to obscure the view. This dust penetrated the utmost recesses of the boys' lungs. A kind of slave-driver sometimes stands over the boys, prodding or kicking them into obedience. South Pittston, Pennsylvania.

HIRAM PULK, age nine, working in a canning company. "I ain't very fast, only about five boxes a day. They pay about five cents a box," he said. Eastport, Maine.

ROB KIDD, one of the young workers in a glass factory. Alexandria, Virginia.

the Short, Dark Life
OF A COAL MINER

In Gary, West Virginia, a boy works ten hours a day applying the brakes on a motor train.

What is historically the deadliest occupation in America?

Police officer? Lion tamer? Skyscraper builder? The answer is actually a coal miner. By 1910 the United States was the largest coal producer in the world. More than 750,000 miners wrestled nearly 550 million tons of coal out of the ground each year. And nearly 105,000 miners died from accidents between 1900 and 2014.

Mining is a difficult and highly dangerous job. A miner may be crushed to death at any time by a falling roof, burned to death by exploding gas, or blown to pieces by a blast. One of the scariest parts of mining is methane, which is a colorless, odorless gas produced by coal. It bursts into flames at the slightest spark.

Considering that miners wore caps with flame lanterns to light their way, the chance for explosion was high. **The job was so dangerous, life insurance companies used to refuse to cover miners.**

In 1907 alone more than 3,200 people were killed working in mines, the most on record.

But the deadliest month of that year for this lethal profession was December, when in a thirty-one-day span, 702 miners were killed in five explosions. That body count is low, as mining companies didn't include the undocumented young boys and old men working there who were killed.

The worst explosion in history occurred December 6 at the

Boys were hired as drivers, guiding the horses that pulled the coal cars, and as trappers, who opened and closed doors, in mines such as this one in Fairmont, West Virginia.

Fairmont Coal Company in Monongah, West Virginia. Twin explosions, which could be heard eight miles away, tore through two mines. Poisonous gas collected in the wrecked mines, which made rescue efforts impossible for nearly a week. By then everyone in the mine was dead. An estimated 362 men and an untold number of boys were killed.

Soon after the explosion at Monongah, four miners emerged through an opening, dazed and bleeding but otherwise unharmed. The stunned survivors could tell nothing of the fate of the others still underground.

THE DEAD THAT NEVER LEAVE THE MINE

In 1900 Winter Quarters was a thriving coal-mining town near Scofield, Utah. Nearly two thousand people lived there, most of them working in a mine considered safe by the standards of the day. But it wasn't safe enough. On May 1, an explosion of blasting powder in a mine tunnel eventually killed 199 men. Not long afterward, the ghost appeared.

On January 17, 1901, the *Eastern Utah Advocate* newspaper reported, "The superstitious miners, who are foreigners, have come to the conclusion that the property is haunted, inhabited by a ghost. Several of them have heard strange and unusual noises, and those favored with a keener vision than their fellow workmen have actually seen a headless man walking about the mine and according to their statements have accosted the ghost and addressed it or he. At other times the headless man would get aboard the coal cars to which mules and horses are worked and ride with the driver to the mouth of the tunnel when he would mysteriously vanish and again reappear in the mine."

Jumping to Escape the Flames AT THE TRIANGLE SHIRTWAIST FACTORY

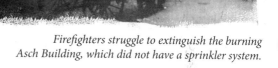

On Saturday afternoon, March 25, 1911, the five hundred mostly female workforce of the Triangle Shirtwaist Factory in New York City were busy sewing and cutting. No alarms went off when a fire broke out on the eighth floor at 4:45. A call was made to the tenth floor but no one thought to let any of the 240 workers on the ninth floor know until it was too late.

Firefighters struggle to extinguish the burning Asch Building, which did not have a sprinkler system.

Flames quickly blocked the stairwell and the elevator ceased to run.

The doors were locked to prevent theft, and the foreman with the key had already bolted for the street.

The fire escape was flimsy and soon gave out under the weight of the women, causing them to fall to their deaths. Firefighters arrived, but their ladders wouldn't go higher than the sixth floor. Other than a few buckets of water, there was nothing to stop the fire from burning the piles of scrap fabric on the factory floor. The workers were trapped.

PROGRESS

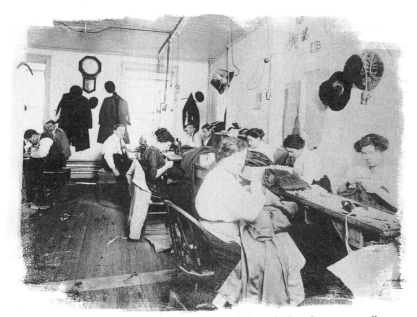
Few workers complained about the long hours or small pay because the job provided much-needed income.

On March 28 the *Chicago Sunday Tribune* reported, "A thirteen-year-old girl hung for three minutes by her finger tips to the sill of a tenth floor window. A tongue of flame licked at her fingers and she dropped into a life net held by firemen. Two women fell into the net at almost the same moment. The strands parted and the two were added to the death list."

So they started to jump. Louis Waldman, among the bystanders that day, later described the scene: "Horrified and helpless, the crowds—I among them—looked up at the burning building, **saw girl after girl appear at the reddened windows, pause for a terrified moment, and then leap to the pavement below, to land as a mangled, bloody pulp**. Occasionally a girl who had hesitated too long was licked by pursuing flames and, screaming with clothing and hair ablaze, plunged like a living torch to the street."

Charles Willis Thompson, a *New York Times* correspondent, later wrote in a letter about covering the fire, "It conveys no picture to the imagination to say that the fire was one hundred feet above the street . . . But when you stand on the street and almost topple over backward craning your neck to see a place away up in the sky, and realize the way those bodies came hurtling down over the inconceivable distance, it seems more as if it were one hundred miles."

The Triangle Shirtwaist Factory Fire was the deadliest workplace accident in New York City's history. By the time the fires in the supposedly fireproof building went out, 146 of the five hundred employees were dead. All but twenty-three were women and nearly half were teenagers. The public outcry led to dozens of new workplace safety laws.

THE UNLOCKING DOOR

While the inferno that swept through the Triangle Shirtwaist Factory killed anyone not lucky enough to escape, it did not destroy the building, which was renovated and eventually bought by New York University. People working there have claimed to smell smoke and see something fall past the window when nothing is there. And doors that were recently locked are found unlocked moments later. Perhaps the spirits are still trying to escape!

The escape route for the 240 employees on the ninth floor was blocked by sewing machines on 75-foot-long tables, back-to-back chairs, and large work baskets in the aisles.

LEADER

A Bullet in His Chest, TEDDY ROOSEVELT KEEPS TALKING

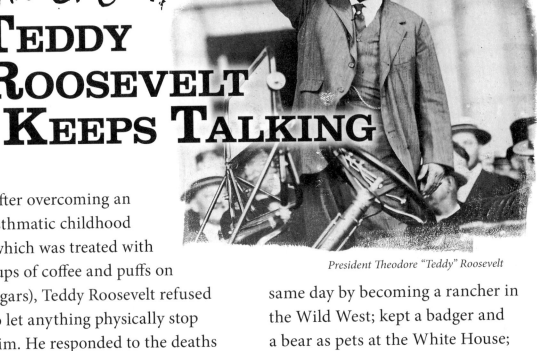

President Theodore "Teddy" Roosevelt

After overcoming an asthmatic childhood (which was treated with cups of coffee and puffs on cigars), Teddy Roosevelt refused to let anything physically stop him. He responded to the deaths of his mother and first wife on the same day by becoming a rancher in the Wild West; kept a badger and a bear as pets at the White House; was blinded in his left eye due to a boxing accident while president; and supposedly confronted a hired killer named E. G. Paddock in North Dakota with the words, **"I understand you have threatened to kill me on sight.**

The gun John Schrank used to shoot Teddy Roosevelt.

I have come over to see when you want to begin the killing."

In 1899 he gave a speech titled "The Strenuous Life," which summed up his life's philosophy, that the "highest form of success comes, not to the man who desires mere easy peace, but to the man who does not shrink from danger, from hardship or from bitter toil, and who out of these wins the splendid ultimate triumph."

Yet what probably cemented Roosevelt's reputation as our country's toughest president was a speech he gave in 1912. He was on the campaign trail for his third term in office for his self-created Bull Moose political party when his train stopped in Milwaukee, Wisconsin. He got into his car and stood up in the backseat to acknowledge the cheering of the crowd. Just then John Schrank, a

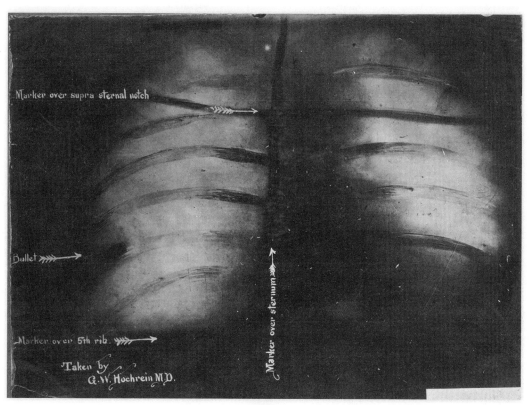

Marker over supra sternal notch

Bullet

Marker over 5th rib.

Taken by
G. W. Hochrein M.D.

Marker over sternum

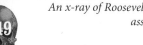

149

An x-ray of Roosevelt's lungs shows where the assassin's bullet was lodged.

disgruntled saloonkeeper, shot Roosevelt. The bullet, slowed by a copy of his speech and eyeglass case in his pocket, pierced his chest.

The *New York Times* reported, "With astonishing courage and despite the fact that he had no idea whether his wound was mortal or not, the colonel insisted on proceeding to the Auditorium and going on with his speech. He said it might be his last chance to get his ideas before the people."

"Friends," Roosevelt said as he began his speech, "I shall ask you to be as quiet as possible. **I don't know whether you fully understand that I have just been shot**—but it takes more than that to **kill a Bull Moose.**" He went on to speak for more than an hour.

After the speech, he was rushed to the hospital, where doctors found a bullet in his ribs that was too dangerous to remove. The *Times* stated, "His splendid physique

ANOTHER TOUGH GUY WHO WASN'T AS LUCKY

Thomas J. Smith was a professional middleweight boxer and police officer in New York City. He gradually moved west, working as a lawman in Wyoming and along the railroad line. He became known for being tough as nails. When he came to Abilene, Kansas, in 1869, it was a lawless cattle town. As marshal he insisted that there be no guns within town limits, taking on outlaws with his fists. A number of people tried to kill him but none were successful. However, he took on more than he could handle when he went to confront two farmers who had murdered a man. They shot Smith in the chest, beat him with a rifle, and then cut his head off!

enabled him to recover quickly from a wound that might have been fatal to an ordinary man."

PART V: THE GREAT WAR AND THE JAZZ AGE (1914–1936)

1914 World War I begins; Panama Canal opens

U.S. enters World War I; Woodrow Wilson begins second term as president **1917**

1919 Women granted the right to vote

Warren G. Harding begins term as president **1921**

1923 Harding dies suddenly; Calvin Coolidge sworn in as president

Coolidge begins second term as president **1925**

1927 Charles Lindbergh completes first solo transatlantic flight

Eight Hundred Drown Ten Feet from the Dock IN THE CHICAGO RIVER

Rescuing those who could clamber to the top of the boat wasn't hard, but that was not the case for those trapped belowdecks.

On the morning of July 24, 1915, the steamship *Eastland* was tied to the dock while passengers boarded. The ship was packed with Western Electric factory workers traveling to a company excursion. As it was cool and rainy, many of the more than 2,500 passengers were belowdecks. Suddenly the ship just rolled over, trapping those below. Water began pouring in.

Writer Jack Woodford witnessed the disaster. In his autobiography he wrote, "I looked across the river. As I watched in disoriented stupefaction a steamer large as an ocean liner slowly turned over on its side as though it were a whale going to take a nap. I didn't believe [it could happen] in excellent weather, with no explosion, no fire, nothing. I thought I had gone crazy."

Helen Repa, a nurse at the Western Electric plant hospital, arrived soon after the ship rolled. She recalled, **"People were struggling in the water, clustered so thickly that they literally covered the surface of the river.** A few were swimming; some clinging to a life raft that had floated free, others clutching at anything that they could reach—at bits of wood, at each other, grabbing each other, pulling each other down, and screaming! The screaming was the most horrible of all."

Marie Linhart was one of the passengers trapped between decks. A welder cut a hole into the hull of the ship, saving her life.

Firefighters and other rescue workers arrived quickly and began cutting into the ship's hold, but they were not quick enough to save many of those trapped below. Here, Chicago fireman Leonard Olson carries the body of a toddler who died in the disaster.

"My fingers were all bruised and bloody, but I held on," she remembered. "A man laid down on the side [of the hull] up there and reached down and grabbed my hands and hiked me up. Looking down, all I could see was hair and hands and feet and picnic baskets and children crying. I thought I was going to get torn back down, people were just grabbing and holding and trying to get out. My skirt was off, my shoes were off, my clothes were torn."

Marie survived but many did not. In water only twenty feet deep, 844 people drowned in the Chicago River. More passengers died that day than the number of passengers who perished in the sinking of the *Titanic*.

TEMPORARY MORGUE, PERMANENT GHOSTS

As many as two hundred of the *Eastland* dead were taken to Chicago's Second Regiment Armory, which became a temporary morgue. "Nearly every room on the lower floors of the warehouse contained bodies," reported a newspaper. "The remaining space was filled with crowds of police-

The temporary morgue at the Second Regiment Armory on Washington Boulevard.

men, rescuers, friends and relatives of the dead, and a corps [group] of fifty embalmers."

Oprah Winfrey established Harpo Studios in the Armory in 1989. Soon after it seemed that the building was haunted by the spirits of the *Eastland* dead. Security guards reported the spooky sounds of children playing, doors slamming, and women sobbing. Others have seen the ghost called the "Gray Lady" floating down hallways in a flowing dress. Her image has even been caught on security cameras! In 1996 Oprah talked about the building's ghosts on her talk show, saying, "That's why I'm not here after midnight."

One Million American Soldiers IN ONE BATTLE

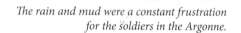

The rain and mud were a constant frustration for the soldiers in the Argonne.

World War I had been raging for three years before the United States joined the fight in April 1917. On September 26, 1918, American soldiers gathered to assault the German-held Meuse-Argonne region of eastern France. In the six-week-long battle, a mind-boggling one million American troops would participate in the offensive.

Many of the American soldiers involved had never been in combat before. Lieutenant "Bud" Bradford Jr., of the U.S. Army's Forty-First Infantry Division,

described the early moments: "We moved into the trenches on the famous hills about Verdun. The ground was plowed in a sickening churn. We dug in, for the trenches were in poor repair. **We dug but not dirt alone—legs, arms, skulls, helmets, all the debris of the mighty struggle.** At two thirty the barrage cut loose. For

Wounded soldiers in an American field hospital set up in the ruins of a church in France.

three hours a solid sheet of flame lit up all behind us. O God, O God, the poor devils on the other end."

Corporal Alvin C. York of the 328th Infantry wrote on October 7, 1918, "We lay in some little holes by the roadside all day . . . Lots of big shells bursting all around us . . . airplanes were buzzing overhead most all the time, just like a lot of hornets. Lots of men were killed by the artillery fire. And lots more wounded . . . The woods were all mussed up and looked as if a terrible cyclone had swept through them. **But God would never be cruel enough to create a cyclone as terrible as that Argonne battle."**

When the battle finally ended at eleven a.m. on November 11 (memorialized as "the eleventh hour of the eleventh day of the eleventh month") with complete German surrender, 120,000 Americans were wounded, including more than 26,000 dead. For American troops the Battle of the Argonne Forest was the largest and bloodiest battle of World War I.

American soldiers transporting German prisoners from the front lines at the Argonne.

NOT CITIZENS BUT SOLDIERS

More than 4.7 million Americans served in World War I. At the time, Native Americans were not legally considered U.S. citizens, so they could not be drafted. However, many volunteered and more than ten thousand served. In 1919 Congress passed an act that conferred citizenship on Native Americans who had served in the war. Native Americans as a whole were not granted legal citizenship until 1924.

A Cherokee soldier at a hospital in France during World War I.

Spanish Influenza Infects
A QUARTER OF ALL AMERICANS

An emergency hospital set up at Camp Funston in Kansas during the epidemic, where one soldier estimated there were between 6,000 and 7,000 influenza cases.

The Spanish Flu Pandemic of 1918 came on like a freight train, killing healthy young people within days of infection. Five percent of victims, many of them soldiers, died when they caught the disease. They turned blue from lack of oxygen, tore muscles from coughing up blood, and finally suffocated on their own bodily fluids.

At the disease's height, more than ten thousand people died each week in some cities. The pandemic, which began in France, killed an estimated fifty million people, a larger number than all who died in World War I. In the United States the flu affected nearly twenty-five percent of the population.

Policemen in Seattle wore paper masks during the epidemic, which offered no real protection from the deadly disease.

Soldiers returning from WWI brought the flu back with them from Europe. Crowded conditions helped it spread. An outbreak in Kansas in March 1918 likely represented some of the first cases in the United States. Dr. Victor Vaughan, stationed at Camp Devens outside of Boston, wrote, "Every bed is full, yet others crowd in. The faces wear a bluish cast; a cough brings up the blood-stained sputum [phlegm]. In the morning, the **dead bodies are stacked about the morgue like cordwood.**" Caskets were in short supply, so the dead were often left for days or sometimes abandoned in the street.

With no cure, many turned to home remedies such as garlic or kerosene on sugar. People wore masks, avoided crowds, and were ticketed for spitting on the streets. Nothing helped. After several months and tens of millions dead worldwide, the disease ran its course and people stopped dying. Doctors never understood why.

The 1918 influenza virus recreated by microbiologists at the National Center for Infectious Disease.

FROZEN CORPSE HELPS FIGHT THE FLU

The flu was killing everyone everywhere, and it made a particularly deadly stop in the small town of Brevig Mission, Alaska, in November 1918. In a short five days, it killed ninety percent of the Inuit population. Piles of dead bodies were eventually thrown into a mass grave by miners paid to bury them in the icy ground. In 1997 scientist Johan Hultin traveled to the village. With the permission of the descendants, he dug up one of the bodies, which had been preserved by the cold. He took a sample of the lung tissue and sent it to scientists who were trying to reconstruct the disease. Hultin's sample made that possible. Today, scientists are trying to determine how to fight the Spanish Influenza, in case it ever comes back.

the Gooey Molasses flood OF BOSTON

The firehouse on Commercial Street was knocked off its foundation by the flood. One firefighter, pinned by debris inside, could not escape and drowned in a pool of molasses.

The rivets on the holding tank on Commercial Street in Boston popped like gunfire in the early afternoon of January 15, 1919. Seconds later **more than two million gallons of molasses were released in a massive wave.** The dense wall of syrup burst from Purity Distilling Company's five-story-tall steel tank and raced through the streets at thirty-five miles per hour, pulling buildings off their foundations. The elevated train girders on Atlantic Avenue snapped like twigs under the weight of twenty-six million pounds of molasses that flooded the waterfront neighborhood. Many people and horses were trapped in the goo that spread

350 feet across and three feet deep.

The *Boston Post* reported, "The sight that greeted the first of the rescuers on the scene is almost indescribable in words. Molasses, waist deep, covered the street and swirled and bubbled about the wreckage. Here and there struggled a form— whether it was animal or human being it was impossible to tell. **Only an upheaval, a thrashing about in a sticky mess, showed where any life was.** Horses died like so many flies on sticky fly paper."

More than 150 people were injured, including nine-year-old Anthony di Stasio. He was lucky to be rescued from a pile of bodies at the morgue, where he had been mistaken for dead. Twenty-one people suffocated in the flood. Fourteen buildings were destroyed, causing property damage of more than $100 million in today's dollars.

As you might guess, the sticky mess was hard to clean up. Fire hoses of seawater forced the sludge into the bay, staining the water brown for months.

The tank was later found to be too weak; it had been built quickly and never tested. The company had even painted the tank brown to hide the frequent leaks!

Wreckage near the elevated train lines included many trucks that were parked underneath.

FLOUR INFERNO

Few people would think to fear molasses. Even fewer would be afraid of flour. Yet workers at Washburn A Mill in Minneapolis, Minnesota, one of the largest flour mills in the world, had reason to be. On May 2, 1878, a spark ignited flour dust in the air of the mill. An eyewitness told a local reporter that he saw flames, "then the windows burst out, the walls cracked between the windows and fell, and the roof was projected into the air to great height, followed by a cloud of black smoke, through which brilliant flashes resembling lightning passing to and fro." The explosion and fireball killed eighteen workers.

Ruins of the Washburn A Mill after the explosion.

CHARLES PONZI, *the Godfather of financial Schemes*

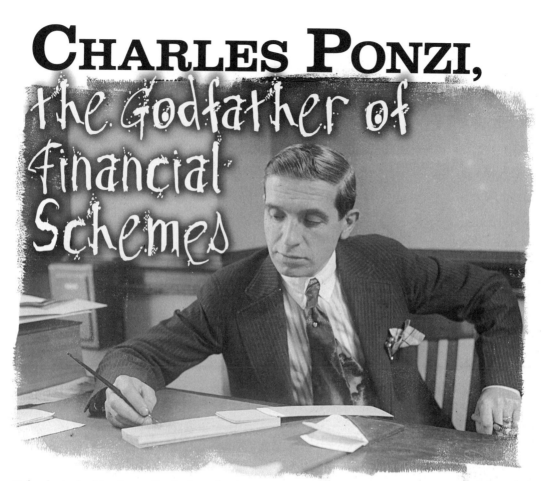

Before beginning his scheme, Charles Ponzi lived in Montreal, Canada, where he went to prison for three years for forging a check, like the one he appears to be writing here.

A "Ponzi scheme" is an investing scam that promises a huge profit with little or no risk to investors. In the scheme, profits for early investors are paid by money acquired from new investors. The plan works as long as more and more new investors sign on and collapses when new investments stop.

This type of financial swindle was named after an Italian businessman and con artist named Charles Ponzi. In 1919 he bought discounted postal coupons for airmail stamps in other countries and redeemed them for face value in the United States. When he realized the money he could make, he began

Ponzi, center, on his way to court, was prosecuted by both the federal government and the state of Massachusetts. He was convicted both times.

recruiting other people. Investors were promised a fifty percent return, meaning they would make all of their invested money back plus fifty percent more, after forty-five days, or a one hundred percent return after ninety days. **At the scheme's height Ponzi was making $250,000 a day.**

In Ponzi's autobiography he quoted the *New York Evening World*: "Whoever said that proud old New Englanders are conservative, undoubtedly made that statement before the advent of Charles Ponzi. Today all Boston is get-rich-quick

mad over him, the creator of fortunes, the modern King Midas who doubles your money in ninety days. . . . He has been doing it for eight months and he is still at it . . . With no other security than his personal note, Boston is pouring all its savings into Ponzi's hands. **Like a tidal wave, the passion for investment with the new Italian banker has swept over Boston folk** until it took half of the Boston police force to subdue the enthusiasm of a throng of prospective investors overflowing from the banking office . . . into the street, blocking the traffic."

Ponzi's newfound wealth did not go unnoticed. A story by the *Boston Post* on July 24,

1920, detailed the investments of the "financial wizard," causing people to flock to his shop.

Less than one month later, Ponzi was arrested, after costing his investors an estimated twenty million dollars (worth approximately $222 million today) and causing the collapse of six banks. He was convicted of mail fraud and received five years of jail time from the federal government and nine years from the state. Upon his release Ponzi was deported. He died penniless in Brazil in 1949.

Ponzi awaiting deportation after serving time in prison.

THE GREAT CRASH OF 1929

In the 1920s, everyone thought they could make quick money in the stock market. And many did, because the value of stocks kept rising. But in 1929 millions of investors lost a fortune when Wall Street's value took a dive. It is considered the most devastating financial crash in the history of the United States. On October 29, what would become known as Black Tuesday, the market lost fourteen billion dollars in a single day. Jonathan Leonard, a reporter, wrote, "Horrified brokers watched the selling orders accumulate. It wasn't a flood; it was a deluge." This was the start of a ten-year financial crisis known as the Great Depression, which plagued America with massive poverty and unemployment.

RADIUM, A CURE that Makes your Jaw Fall Off

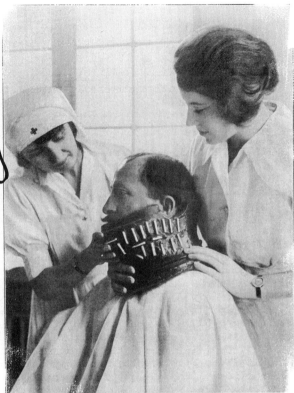

In hopes of a cure, tubes with small doses of radium are strapped onto a man with cancer.

"The Radium Water Worked Fine Until His Jaw Came Off," read the headline of the *Wall Street Journal* article about Eben Byers, who was chairman of the A. M. Byers Steel Company and an amateur golf champion. He was also a huge fan of William J. A. Bailey's Radithor, a tonic made with radium—a type of radioactive metal—said to provide a metabolic kick to the body's endocrine system, as well as cure 160 different conditions. In 1928 he began drinking at least two bottles a day, which he told friends and associates made him feel great.

The use of radium to treat listlessness and other conditions was a trend in the 1920s.

Beyond drinks, it was found in toothpaste, face creams, and

Radione tablets, which people ate for energy.

hair tonics. By 1930 the Federal Trade Commission began to realize that radium was not harmless. We now know that it gives off radiation, which can injure or destroy living cells. If consumed it builds up in bones and damages tissue. In 1931 the FTC asked Byers to testify but he was too sick. **By then his upper and lower jaw had been removed and he had holes in his skull.** He died in 1932.

GLOW-IN-THE-DARK DEATH

Radium glows a blue-green without any power source. Manufacturers soon realized that it was perfect for watch faces. The U.S. Radium Corporation immediately hired women in Illinois to put the numbers on with radium paint. They were paid about five cents a watch, and they did about two hundred watches a day. However, to paint the small numbers, the women had to get sharp points on their brushes, so they'd lick the tips. This caused the women to ingest unsafe amounts of radium. Their bones developed holes in them, causing their teeth to fall out and their legs to break. By 1927 more than fifty women had died from radium poisoning.

For the low price of $1, your family can be poisoned by a set of cookware made of clay and radium!

Machine-Gunning Miners
at the BATTLE AT
BLAIR MOUNTAIN

The miners wore red bandannas and were given the nickname "red necks,"
which is now slang for a working-class person from a rural area.

Imagine facing a private army of two thousand men with machine guns and planes that could drop bleach and shrapnel bombs. This is what greeted the miners in Logan County, West Virginia, when they marched on Blair Mountain in an attempt to create a union. It became the most violent labor confrontation in American history.

Miners faced death daily doing a job that paid little compared to the risks. Much of the money they did earn went back to the mining company. They rented company tools necessary for their job, ate food from the company store, and lived in company houses. A union was a way for miners to bargain for better working conditions. Bill Blizzard, a union organizer, wrote in *When Miners March*, "Let it be most solemnly and emphatically stated . . . that the thousands of miners assembled for their now-famous march to Blair Mountain were no armed hoodlums intent on plunder, murder, and assorted villainy. These were men of the same stamp as those . . . who suffered with Washington at Valley Forge."

Fearful of losing money, the mine companies hired the Baldwin-Felts Detective Agency to intimidate the miners so they wouldn't join the union. They beat up people, evicted them from their homes, and even ran armored trains through tent cities. The miners retaliated until there was bloodshed on both sides, including the

BREAKER BOYS OF THE MINES

Between 1865 and 1920 thousands of boys between the ages of eight and twelve years old worked in mines. These "breaker boys" separated coal from other rock by hand. Laws passed in the 1880s prohibited workers younger than twelve years old at the mines. However, the laws were rarely enforced.

Breaker boys typically worked ten hours a day, six days a week, hunched over a conveyor belt. In 1902 they were paid an average of seventy-five cents a day. "Sitting in a stooping position amid clouds of coal dust is painful, and tiny fingers are cruelly cut and bled by contact with the pieces of coal, which are as sharp as bits of broken glass," the *New York Times* reported in 1885. Many lost fingers, limbs, and even their lives after being caught in the coal breaker machinery.

The noon break at the Pennsylvania Coal Company in 1911.

death of pro-union sheriff Sid Hatfield.

Rising tensions led to a march of 13,000 miners on the capital. The governor rejected the miners' demands. On August 25, 1921, they marched on to Blair Mountain to face the two thousand union-busting, heavily armed troops led by Sheriff Don Chafin. For days they battled, firing one million rounds of ammunition. More than fifty people were killed. When President Harding threatened to send in troops, the miners fled. Many were later tried for treason, though few went to jail. While they did not win the right to unionize, the uprising did bring their plight to the nation's attention.

Fighting against the miners was an army of sheriff's deputies, mine guards, store clerks, and state police.

THE **TRI-STATE TORNADO'S** *trail of Death*

The tornado's path passed through the town of Princeton, Indiana, decimating it.

The deadliest tornado day in the deadliest tornado year was March 18, 1925.

For three and a half hours on that day, the Tri-State Tornado tore through Missouri, Illinois, and Indiana at sixty-two miles per hour. It created the longest tornado path ever recorded in the world—219 miles.

"All morning, before the tornado, it had rained. The day was dark and gloomy. The air was heavy. There was no wind. Then the drizzle increased. The heavens seemed to open, pouring down a flood," wrote a reporter in the *St. Louis Post-Dispatch*. "The day grew black, then the air was filled with ten thousand things. Boards, poles, cans, garments, stoves, whole sides of the little frame houses, in some cases the houses themselves, were picked up and smashed to earth. And living beings, too. A baby was blown from its mother's arms. **A cow, picked up by the wind, was hurled into the village restaurant."**

With no warning system in place, people scrambled to find shelter before the nearly mile-wide black cloud was upon them. Beginning in Missouri at 12:40 p.m., the tornado killed eleven people before crossing the Mississippi River into Illinois at 2:30, killing 613 people, and ended its run in Indiana at 4:38, leaving seventy-one dead. Murphysboro, Illinois, lost 234 people and 170 of its two hundred city blocks from the tornado and the ensuing fires.

Paul South, a teenager in De Soto, Illinois, remembered when the tornado hit his high school: "It got real dark and I heard a noise like a million trains. The kids all around me started screaming and crying . . . Then the bricks began to fall . . . I opened my eyes and saw [kids] being buried beneath the bricks. Some of them had their arms raised as the bricks fell." His classmate Garrett Crews stated, "Down in the northeast corner . . . there was a girls' toilet. And I recall seeing a girl come out of the toilet— the wind picked her up, just head-high or so, and blew her more or less straight to the fence on the north side of our school building. She was found dead in the fence."

In that single day, 695 people were killed, more than two thousand were injured, and fifteen thousand homes were destroyed.

TOP FIVE DEADLIEST TORNADOES

1. 1925 - Missouri, Illinois, and Indiana - Death toll: 695
2. 1840 - Mississippi - Death toll: 317
3. 1896 - Missouri and Illinois - Death toll: 255
4. 1936 - Tupelo, Mississippi - Death toll: 216
5. 1936 - Gainesville, Florida - Death toll: 203

Gainesville, Florida

THE 23,000-SQUARE-MILE
Mississippi River Flood

By May, the Mississippi River below Memphis, seen here, swelled to 60 miles wide. Charles French, a boy at the time, said, "I remember seeing houses floating downstream with only their roofs above water."

In April 1927 the rains wouldn't stop. In New Orleans it rained fifteen inches in eighteen hours. The Mississippi River's protective levees built to hold in the water began to collapse just south of Cairo, Illinois. The river, carrying three million cubic feet of water a second, flooded thousands of farms and hundred of towns. Covering nearly twenty-seven thousand square miles in seven states, the flood left nearly 600,000 people homeless. The Red Cross had a task,

the director said, "the magnitude of which staggers the imagination." They set up 154 camps in the area, feeding 325,000 people for nearly five months, all on donations from the American people.

Secretary of Commerce Herbert Hoover, who was placed in charge of flood relief by President Calvin Coolidge, visited ninety-one communities by train. In each, his message was the same: "A couple of thousand refugees are coming. They've got to have

A refugee camp on high ground near Vicksburg, Mississippi, where the river was 80 miles wide.

accommodations. Huts. Water mains. Sewers. Streets. Dining halls. Meals. Doctors. Everything. And you haven't got months to do it. You haven't got weeks. You've got hours." And citizens responded, along with a huge effort by the Red Cross.

In Greenville, Mississippi, the town was covered by ten feet of water. Nearly thirteen thousand evacuees, mostly African Americans, were stranded in a seven-mile-long camp on an eight-foot-wide levee for days without food or clean water. **They were not allowed to evacuate and were forced to rebuild the levees for little pay.** W. A. Percy, the Chairman of Relief in the town, issued a statement that read, "All negroes in Greenville outside of the levee camp who are able to work should work. If work is offered them and they refuse to work, they should be arrested as vagrants. Names and addresses of those refusing to work should be telephoned to police headquarters. I suggest one dollar a day as a fair wage at this time." Disgusted by the treatment and with their homes destroyed, many African Americans moved north after the flood receded.

THE JOHNSTOWN FLOOD

On May 31, 1889, Pennsylvania's South Fork Dam burst. Twenty million tons of water raced toward Johnstown, smashing into it at forty miles per hour. Telegraph Operator D. M. Montgomery described it as "a mountain of water coming down, full of trees, houses, and everything; and the water seemed to be rolling over and over, and just crushing everything in front of it. If it struck anything, you never saw it after that." Everything in the flood's path was destroyed and 2,209 people were killed.

There was so much flooding that it took two months for the Mississippi River water to return to normal levels.

the Deadly Collapse
OF THE ST. FRANCIS DAM

An aerial view shows the broken water barrier of San Francisquito Canyon after the dam burst.

At three minutes to midnight on March 12, 1928, the seven-hundred-foot-long St. Francis Dam in Los Angeles County collapsed, causing more than twelve billion gallons of water to surge down the San Francisquito Canyon in an hour. This caused a 140-foot-high wave that traveled west at eighteen miles per hour, leveling everything in its path. More than six hundred people were killed as the wall of water traveled fifty-four miles to finally empty into the Pacific Ocean five and a half hours later.

Ray Rising, one of the few survivors, later remembered, **"I hear a roaring like a cyclone. The water was so high we couldn't get out the front door. The house disintegrated.**

176

In the darkness I became tangled with an oak tree, fought clear and swam to the surface."

The next day the *Oakland Tribune* wrote, "Looking down the valley, **where yesterday had bloomed numbers of little citrus groves, there was nothing to be seen but bare expanse of yellow sand,** spread on top of the soil some places to a depth of thirty feet by the advancing wall of water . . . not a single structure remained standing, except a lone powerhouse . . . In one eddy of the stream floated the floors of two houses, the superstructure of both having been carried away in the midnight horror of water."

On March 14, the *Los Angeles Times* reported, "Many bodies were buried underneath tightly packed mud. Victims were trapped while they slept, clad only in night clothes. Hurled

along on the twisting flood, their bodies were buffeted about, making identification in many cases almost impossible."

Who was to blame for the massive loss of life and more than seven million dollars in property

Before

After

A massive gravity dam, the St. Francis was designed to hold back water using its sheer weight alone. A landslide caused the water to be released, devastating sixty-five miles of valley.

damage? Fingers pointed at William Mulholland, Los Angeles's superintendent of water, who had overseen the building of the dam, as well as the city's complex water system. At the trial he rose and said, "Don't blame anyone else, you just fasten it on me. If there was an error in human judgment, I was the human, and I won't try to fasten it on anyone else. **On occasion like this, I envy the dead."**

While he was never formally charged, he was still blamed, though it was later determined that the cause of the collapse was something he could not have prevented.

With the amount of concrete used to build the Hoover Dam, you could build a 4-foot-wide sidewalk around all of Earth at the equator.

BURIED IN HOOVER DAM

How did the rumor that workers are buried in the cement of the Hoover Dam start? More than one hundred men died during the building of the dam. A ton of concrete was poured to make Hoover more than sixty stories high and as wide as two football fields. It seems logical that at least one person would fall in. However, the cement blocks that make up the dam were poured in thin layers, so they could not actually contain the dead. Still, one fact about the dead is odd: In 1922, one of the first to die was J. G. Tierney, who drowned in the Colorado River while surveying the water. Thirteen years later, his son, Patrick, became the last person to die during construction when he fell from an intake tower.

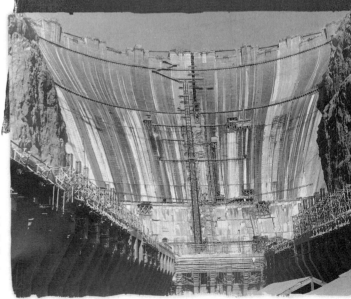

Black Sunday,
A DEVASTATING DUST STORM

Avis Carlson wrote of the storm, "We live with the dust, eat it, sleep with it, watch it strip us of possessions and the hope of possessions."

When farmers cultivated the Great Plains in the 1910s and 1920s, their plows pulled up the deep-rooted grasses that kept the topsoil in place. Drought and high winds combined to put that soil into the air, causing what was known as the Dust Bowl of the 1930s. Beyond finding its way into every crack or crevice, the dirt was also dangerous. Cars driven through dust storms had to drag chains behind them to ground them in the static electricity. Those who breathed in the airborne particles could be struck with dust pneumonia, which killed hundreds.

One of the worst dust storms in history took place on April 14, 1935. **Hundreds of thousands of tons of soil clouded the air, creating a black blizzard** that hit the country from the Dakotas to

Musician Woody Guthrie wrote a song about the storm, which included the line:
"It fell across our city like a curtain of black rolled down."

Texas. The Weather Bureau in Dodge City, Kansas, reported: **"The onrushing cloud, the darkness, and the thick, choking dirt, made this storm one of terror and the worst, while it lasted, ever known here."** Rising some five hundred feet high and traveling at nearly sixty miles per hour, the churning walls of dirt generated massive amounts of static electricity, causing people to experience huge electric shocks and engines to stall.

Pauline Winkler Grey, who saw the storm coming from her living room window in Kansas, described it as "a mammoth

waterfall in reverse . . . the apex [highest part] of the cloud was plumed and curling, seething and tumbling over itself from north to south and whipping trash, papers, sticks, and cardboard cartons before it . . .

As the wall of dust and sand struck our house, the sun was instantly blotted out completely. Gravel particles clattered against the windows and pounded down on the roof. The floor shook with the impact of the wind . . . We stood in our living room in pitch blackness."

When the rains stopped in 1931, the Southern Plains endured ten years of powerful dust storms, each carrying millions of tons of stinging, blinding black dirt.

Clyde Barrow and Bonnie Parker

THE DUST BOWL BANDITS: BONNIE AND CLYDE

With farmers unable to work the land, many lost their homes and farms to the banks that held the mortgages. This led to widespread resentment against the financial industry. Desperate times led to people romanticizing the bank robbers of the era. None captured the imagination more than young outlaws Clyde Barrow and Bonnie Parker. While some thought they were Robin Hoods who stole from rich institutions, they actually tended to rob from small stores. They also committed as many as thirteen murders. They were gunned down attempting to escape an ambush by lawmen, who fired more than 130 rounds into their stolen car, killing them both. Both of their bodies had so many holes in them, they were difficult to embalm—the fluid kept running out!

DR. FREEMAN'S
Lobotomobile

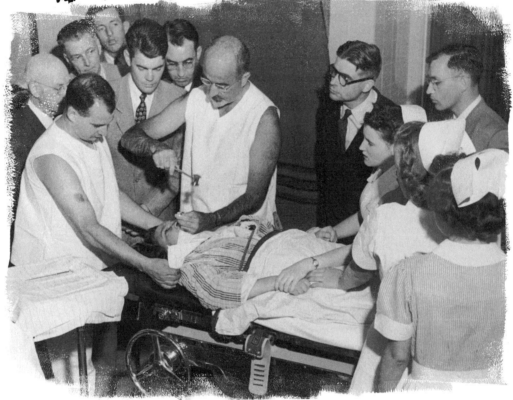

Dr. Freeman performing a lobotomy in 1949 for a crowd of onlookers.
The operating area isn't sterile and the nurse is just holding the patient's arm down.

Dr. Walter Freeman thought he had found the magic treatment to cure people of major mental problems. He called it a lobotomy. He would take a pointed ice pick, which looked like a sharpened screwdriver, and hammer it into a thin part of the skull in the eye socket. Once he was through the bone, Freeman would move the object around in the frontal lobe of the brain, cutting brain pathways. This was supposed to limit the intense ranges of emotion and hallucinations suffered by people with mental illnesses. Sometimes it worked, sometimes not.

The surgery didn't always work because Dr. Freeman didn't really know what he was doing. He wasn't a surgeon. Doctors at that time weren't sure how the brain worked. But there weren't any drugs invented yet that could help, so desperate people would try anything to stop feeling crazy, even if it might kill them. Approximately one-third of the people who had the operation died.

Alice Hammatt was the first patient to receive a lobotomy in the United States. Freeman worked with a surgeon on this operation, which was successful. When she woke, "her face presented a placid expression," Freeman wrote. "By evening she was quite alert, manifested no anxiety or apprehension." The *Washington Star* called the lobotomy "one of the greatest surgical innovations of this generation."

As years passed Freeman stopped working with surgeons

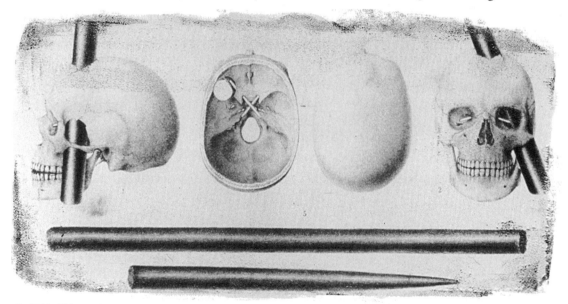

In 1848, Phineas Gage was working construction when an explosive charge sent a piece of iron through his skull and into his brain. He survived, but the accident had given him a type of lobotomy and sparked interest in neuroscience.

and started to perform the operations himself. Soon he was teaching others how to do it, saying, "Any damned fool, even a hospital psychiatrist, could learn it within an afternoon." He seemed to take pride in how quickly he could perform a lobotomy, sometimes doing as many as twenty in a day. He got careless, not wearing gloves or a mask and allowing reporters in to watch the procedure.

He accidentally killed one patient when he stopped mid-operation to pose for a photo.

Freeman heavily promoted the procedure, and the number of lobotomies performed annually increased from 150 in 1945 to more than five thousand in 1949. He even lobotomized nineteen children under the age of eighteen, including a four-year-old. One child was Howard Dully, who was twelve years old when he had the operation. He woke up from surgery in pain with swollen and bruised eyes, later saying,

"I was in a mental fog. I was like a zombie; I had no awareness of what Freeman had done . . .

I didn't want to know any more about it because I was concerned that there might have been some reason that I did deserve this. That's what I was afraid of. What had I . . . done that I don't know about that one would deserve this?"

By 1967 Dr. Freeman had performed more than 2,900 lobotomies, traveling the country in a van known as the lobotomobile. One of his last patients died of a brain hemorrhage during the operation, and Freeman was no longer allowed to work as a doctor. When a new drug called Thorazine began being used to treat mental patients, lobotomies ended because they were too risky. Today lobotomies are used in rare cases when a patient's seizures are so bad that they risk brain damage. But don't worry, none of today's surgeons use ice picks!

WORST DIET PILL EVER

People at the end of the nineteenth century worried about their weight, too. They just came up with some gross ways to fix it. Besides the very dangerous arsenic pill, which could kill you because it was literally poison, another diet remedy was tapeworms. These flatworms are parasites that infect you when you eat undercooked meat containing their eggs. The worm then attaches itself in your intestines, living off the food you eat. Some can grow as big as sixty-five feet long! In the late nineteenth and early twentieth centuries, diet ads promoted easy-to-swallow pills containing tapeworm eggs as a way to fight fat. Once the dieter reached the desired weight, they took a pill that killed the worm. Then they pooped it out . . . unless its eggs had moved to other parts of the body, such as the liver, heart, eyes, or brain, which could be deadly.

SELECTED SOURCES

Deary, Terry. *Horrible Histories: USA*. New York: Scholastic, 2013.

Farquhar, Michael. *Foolishly Forgotten Americans: Pirates, Skinflints, Patriots, and Other Colorful Characters Stuck in the Footnotes of History*. New York: Penguin Group, 2008.

Farquhar, Michael. *A Treasury of Great American Scandals: Tantalizing True Tales of Historic Misbehavior by the Founding Fathers and Others Who Let Freedom Swing*. New York: Penguin Group, 2003.

Normal, Michael and Beth Scott. *Historic Haunted America*. New York: Tor Books, 1995.

Sass, Erik. *Mental Floss History of the United States: The (Almost) Complete and (Entirely) Entertaining Story of America*. New York: HarperCollins Publishers, 2010.

Taylor, Troy and Rene Kruse. *And Hell Followed With It: History & Hauntings of American Disasters*. Decatur, Ill.: Whitechapel Press, 2010.

Taylor, Troy and Rene Kruse. *A Pale Horse Was Death: More American Hauntings and Horrors*. Decatur, Ill.: Whitechapel Press, 2012.

PHOTO CREDITS

Shutterstock, Inc.; 27: Library of Congress; 28: Library of Congress; 29: Library of Congress; 30 top: Everett Historical/Shutterstock, Inc.; 30 bottom: North Wind Picture Archives; 31: Library of Congress; 32: Library of Congress; 33: Benson Lossing/Wikimedia; 34: Library of Congress; 35: North Wind Picture Archives; 36: The Granger Collection; 37: North Wind Picture Archives; 38 top left: Library of Congress; 38 top right: North Wind Picture Archives; 38 bottom: MPI/Getty Images; 39 top: North Wind Picture Archives; 39 bottom: Everett Historical/Shutterstock, Inc.; 40 top: Library of Congress; 40 bottom: Library of Congress; 41: Library of Congress; 42 top: JerryBKeane/iStockphoto; 42 bottom: Niday Picture Library/Alamy Images; 43: MPI/Getty Images; 44 top: North Wind Picture Archives; 44-45 bottom: Library of Congress; 46 top: North Wind Picture Archives; 46-47 wagon wheel: Dhi6un/Dreamstime; 47 top frame: Tudor Stanica/Dreamstime; 47 top portrait: Courtesy Daniel Guggisberg; 48: North Wind Picture Archives; 49 top: Marzolino/Shutterstock, Inc.; 49 bottom: Chip Clark/Dreamstime; 50 top: North Wind Picture Archives; 50 bottom: Anne Chadwick Williams, The Sacramento Bee/AP Images; 51: Wyoming State Archives, Department of State Parks and Cultural Resources; 52: Nawrocki/The Image Works; 53: The British Library Board, 10411.bb.21; 54: aabejon/Getty Images; 55: Cumberland County Historical Society, Carlisle, PA; 56: The Granger Collection; 57: Niday Picture Library/Alamy Images; 58: Lee Foster/Alamy Images; 59 top: Everett Historical/Shutterstock, Inc.; 59 bottom portrait: Library of Congress; 59 bottom frame: Visivasnc/Thinkstock; 60: Library of Congress; 61: Everett Historical/Shutterstock, Inc.; 62: Library of Congress; 63 bottom: Library of Congress; 63 top right: Library of Congress; 63 top left: National Archives and Records Administration; 64: Corbis Images/Getty Images; 65: The Miriam and Ira D. Wallach Division of Art, Prints and Photographs: Photography Collection, The New York Public Library. Pemberton mill. Retrieved from http://digitalcollections.nypl.org/items/510d47e0-709e-a3d9-e040-e00a18064a99; 66: Courtesy of the Lawrence Public Library; 67: The Granger Collection; 68 bottom: Stocksnapper/Dreamstime; 68 top: Library of Congress; 69 top: The Granger Collection; 69 bottom: Library of Congress; 70: National Archives and Records Administration; 71 top: Library of Congress; 71 bottom: National Archives and Records Administration; 72: The Granger Collection; 73: The Granger Collection; 75: The Granger Collection; 76: Library of Congress; 78 top: North Wind Picture Archives; 78-79 barbed wire: Claudio Divizia/Shutterstock, Inc.; 79 top: Library of Congress; 80: Library of Congress; 81: Library of Congress; 82 top: Library of Congress; 82 bottom: Library of Congress; 83 top: Library of Congress; 83 bottom: Library of Congress; 84: The Granger Collection; 85: Library of Congress; 86: Library of Congress; 87: National Numismatic Collection, National Museum of American History/Wikimedia; 88: Library of Congress; 89: Library of Congress; 90: Library of Congress; 91: Hawaii State Archives; 92: Hawaii State Archives; 93: Bettmann/Corbis Images/Getty Images; 94, 95 bottom: Museum of the City of New York/Jacob A. Riis; 95 top: Nina Leen/The LIFE Picture Collection/Getty Images; 96 top left: Library of Congress; 96 top right: Library of Congress; 96 bottom: Library of Congress; 97: Library of Congress; 98 top: Chicago History Museum (ICHi63867); 98 bottom: PhotoQuest/Getty Images; 99 bottom: Chicago History Museum/Getty Images; 99 top: ZU_09/iStockphoto; 100: Minnesota Historical Society; 101 top frame: Chris Chandler/Dreamstime; 101 top portrait: The Granger Collection; 101 bottom: Morphart Creation/Shutterstock, Inc.; 102 top: North Wind Picture Archives; 102 bottom: Denis Kozlenko/iStockphoto; 103: Library of Congress; 104: Library of Congress; 105: Library of Congress; 106: Hulton Archive/Getty Images; 107: Courtesy of Crystal Spivey; 108: Courtesy of The New York Academy of Medicine; 109: AP Images; 110: Library of Congress; 111: Buyenlarge/Getty Images; 112: Brooklyn Public Library -- Brooklyn Collection; 113: Kansas State Historical Society/ZUMAPRESS/Newscom; 114: Ann Ronan Pictures/Getty Images; 115: Pamela Talbird; 116 top: Library of Congress; 116 bottom: Pinkerton Intellectual Property; 117: Library of Congress; 118: Library of Congress; 119 top: Library of Congress; 119 bottom: Library of Congress; 120: Library of Congress; 121: Museum of the City of New York/Getty Images; 122: Naval History and Heritage Command; 123: Library of Congress; 124: Library of Congress; 125: Library of Congress; 126 top: Chicago History Museum/Getty Images; 126 bottom, 127: Library of Congress; 128: AP Images; 129 top left: Library of Congress; 129 top right: Library of Congress; 130: Mary Evans/The Image Works; 131 top: AP Images; 131 bottom: Liszt Collection/Getty Images; 132: Manuscripts and Archives Division, The New York Public Library. (1855). Steamer 'Gen. Slocum' June 15, 1904 [above]; North Brothers Island, East River, N.Y. [below]. Retrieved from http://digitalcollections.nypl.org/items/510d47e1-4434-a3d9-e040-e00a18064a99; 133: Manuscripts and Archives Division, The New York Public Library. (1855). Steamer 'Gen. Slocum' June 15, 1904 [above]; North Brothers Island, East River, N.Y. [below]. Retrieved from http://digitalcollections.nypl.org/items/510d47e1-4434-a3d9-e040-e00a18064a99; 134 top: Library of Congress; 134 bottom, 135 left: The National Archives; 135 right: Library of Congress; 136: Library of Congress; 137: General Research Division, The New York Public Library. (1902 - 1937). Typhoid Mary. Retrieved from http://digitalcollections.nypl.org/items/85674452-ba9e-6934-e040-e00a180606cf; 138 top: AP Images; 138 bottom: Library of Congress; 139: Library of Congress; 140 top: Library of Congress; 140 center: Library of Congress; 140 bottom: Library of Congress; 141 top: Library of Congress; 141 center: Library of Congress; 141 bottom: Library of Congress; 142: Lewis W. Hine/Getty Images; 143: Universal History Archive/UIG/Getty Images; 144: West Virginia Archives and History; 145, 146: Kheel Center for Labor-Management, Cornell University; 147: Brown Brothers; 148 top: Library of Congress; 148 bottom: Harlingue/Getty Images; 149: Houghton Library, Harvard University; 150: Kansas State Historical Society; 151 top left: Library of Congress; 151 top right: Library of Congress; 151 bottom: Library of Congress; 152: AP Images; 153: Jun Fujita/Getty Images; 154: Chicago Tribune historical photo/TNS/Getty Images; 155: Universal History Archive/UIG/Getty Images; 156: Library of Congress; 157 top: Library of Congress; 157 bottom: Universal History Archive/UIG/Getty Images; 158 top: National Museum of Health and Medicine/AFIP/Army.mil; 158 bottom: Atlas Archive/The Image Works; 159 right: Cynthia Goldsmith/Center for Disease Control; 159 left: Atlas Archive/The Image Works; 160: Courtesy of the Boston Public Library, Leslie Jones Collection; 161: Courtesy of the Boston Public Library, Leslie Jones Collection; 162: Minnesota Historical Society/Edward Augustus Bromley; 163: Courtesy of the Boston Public Library, Leslie Jones Collection; 164: Courtesy of the Boston Public Library, Leslie Jones Collection; 165 bottom: Courtesy of the Boston Public Library, Leslie Jones Collection; 165 top: Syracuse Newspapers/The Image Works; 166 top: Mary Evans Picture Library/The Image Works; 166 bottom: John B. Carnett/Bonnier Corp./Getty Images; 167 top: Daily Herald Archive/Getty Images; 167 bottom: Library of Congress; 168: West Virginia Archives and History; 169: Library of Congress; 170: West Virginia Archives and History; 171: Archive Farms/Getty Images; 172: Bettmann/Corbis Images/Getty Images; 173: Mary Evans Picture Library/The Image Works; 174: The Granger Collection; 175 bottom: Everett Historical/Shutterstock, Inc.; 175 top: Library of Congress; 176: AP Images; 177 top: USGS; 177 bottom: USGS; 178: Scherl/The Image Works; 179: Transcendental Graphics/Getty Images; 180 top: Everett Historical/Shutterstock, Inc.; 180-181 bottom: Everett Historical/Shutterstock, Inc.; 181 top: Hulton Archive/Getty Images; 182: Bettman Archives/Corbis Images/Getty Images; 183: The National Library of Medicine; 184: DonGar/Thinkstock; 186: The Natural History Museum/The Image Works.

ABOUT THE AUTHOR

Photo by Claire Williams

DINAH WILLIAMS is an editor and children's book author who is fascinated by odd and unusual stories. Her nonfiction books include *Abandoned Amusement Parks*; *Secrets of Walt Disney World*; *Haunted Hollywood*; and *Spooky Cemeteries*, which won the 2009 Children's Choice Award. She lives in Cranford, NJ, with her husband and daughters, who hate all things scary.